Secret Meanings

Of

Flowers

Including Trees, Shrubs, Vines and Herbs

Brenda Jenkins Kleager

Treasured Secrets Publishing Company

Copyright © 2013 by Brenda Jenkins Kleager

Treasured Secrets Publishing Company
Huntsville, Alabama

ISBN: 978-0979376436

2nd Printing

TABLE OF CONTENTS

DEDICATION

Rick – my husband, who put up with a lot of pizzas and weird dinners, yet still managed to support my efforts

Andy – our son, who helped out with computer questions

Savannah – our daughter, and her husband, Zach, who encouraged me from afar

Shirley, Linda, Ross and Leah – family members who believed in me

Kim – neighbor and friend who served as a sounding board and cheerleader

Laura Stone – editor who helped me turn a garbled mess into a cohesive and useful work

INTRODUCTION

Are you sending the wrong messages with the flowers you select?

With this book, discover the perfect flowers for a variety of needs and occasions. When a friend has a birthday, consider sending pink carnations, pink roses, a willow tree, zinnias, or any of several other plants.

If you want to create a peace-themed garden, you would do well to include violets, oregano, cattails, and a hazel tree.

You will probably not read this book from front to back. In fact, I bet you have already looked up your favorite flower or thumbed through the meanings. Please treat my research as a reference. Use the sections that are of the most benefit to you or your clients.

I have organized the content of this book into two main sections. Section one is an alphabetical list of meanings, emotions, and sentiments with the associated flowers and other plants.

The second section is an alphabetical list of flowers and plants with associated meanings, emotions and sentiments.

Following those sections, I have given you lists of Birth Month Flowers and Anniversary Flowers.

The page about Color Theory provides a safe go-to when you are not sure what flowers to use or to send. Colors also affect mood and intent in your life, such as what you wear or what color scheme you create for your home.

I enjoyed writing the last portion of the book, Flowers and Plants for Special Occasions. The content in this section offers ideas for Weddings, Sympathy, Father's Day, New Home Joy and over thirty more events. These collections will be of value to florists and garden center owners, as well as those of you who enjoy giving flowers.

If you plan to use this reference work often, I suggest that you take a copy to an office supply store. They can cut off the spine and make the book a handy spiral-bound one very inexpensively. I left the margins wide for this purpose.

Why are there contradictory meanings for some of the flowers and plants listed? The reason is relatively simple: the correspondences have been taken from a variety of sources from different time periods. For example a yellow rose meant jealousy or a broken heart during Victorian times, but today it is a symbol for joy, probably because of the color. I have included almost all associations that I found during my research for each plant.

Whether you use this book for practical purposes or for an amusing diversion, I hope you will find *Secret Meanings of Flowers: Including Trees, Shrubs, Vines and Herbs* informative, helpful and fun to read.

BJK

BRIEF HISTORY OF FLOWER AND PLANT MEANINGS

Wreaths of flowers which have meanings range from ancient times to the present.

Early Etruscans, dating from about 700 BC, wore wreaths of ivy, laurel, oak and other plants as crowns.

Later in ancient Greece and Rome, wreaths made from a variety of plant materials were often used to indicate a person's occupation, social status or achievements.

Laurel wreaths worn to represent victory come from a Greek myth about the god Apollo. Today, as at the first Olympics, the laurel wreath is a symbol of victory.

In modern times, we hang wreaths at Advent and other seasonal celebrations. Funeral wreaths are common, as well as wreaths of various styles that we hang on the doors of our homes. Mid-summer festivities throughout Europe and Scandinavia include wreaths of flowers worn by young, unmarried women.

Wreaths were not the only floral arrangement to arise with deep meanings attached. Twelfth century French heraldry gave us the fleur-de-lis as an association with purity when it was thought that an angel gave a lily to Louis VII. The fleur-de-lis remains an important symbol, especially in France.

During the thirteenth century, the rose became a distinctive symbol in England, signifying royalty. Different types and colorations of roses became associated with specific localities (such as York and Lancaster).

Later, the concept of plants having meanings showed up in Shakespeare's *Hamlet* in the early 1600s when he wrote "There's Rosemary, that's for remembrance ... and there is pansies, that's for thoughts."

In the 1700s two Europeans visiting Turkey witnessed *Salam*, the idea of attributing meanings to flowers and objects as a way to express sentiments. Each item had a specific significance and was placed in a small box for delivery much as we would mail a package today. Most of these were intended as love letters. When Lady Mary Wortley Montagu and Seigneur Aubry de la Mettraye returned to Europe, they introduced *Salam* to the French. Soon Germany and England picked up the popular practice. The English passion for gardening led to using flowers and plants to express feelings.

By the mid-1800s and early 1900s, numerous books appeared as an attempt to standardize plant meanings. Naturally, the content of some of these books varied greatly. It was not unusual to own and consult more than one source when trying to discover the meaning of a certain flower. Because this was during Victorian times, the volumes were often quite beautiful. The fact that tens of thousands of these handbooks were sold proves the popularity of the concept, especially in England.

Society's mores at the time practically forbid intimate conversations between young couples; they "spoke" their feelings for each other through bouquets of flowers called "tussie-mussies." It was not unusual for girlfriends to give each other tussie-mussies. In addition, a girl might carry her own bouquet sending her thoughts or mood to those around her. Thus, "The Language of Flowers" was born.

Based on this new "language," when receiving flowers in any form, the recipient needed to consider not only the sentiments of the flowers received, but also where the bow was tied that held the flowers together. If the ribbon was knotted on the right, it meant that the flower meanings were intended as a message about the receiver. If the ribbon was knotted on the left, the flower messages were intended as thoughts from the giver to the receiver.

Similarly, flowers leaning to the right showed that the meaning was "I" and flowers leaning to the left meant "you." Plants presented upside down indicated the opposite of their usual associations.

If the recipient took the flowers with the right hand, it was a positive sign. However accepting the flowers with the left hand meant disagreement.

A young woman who wore flowers over her heart showed love. If she wore them in her hair, caution was indicated. And if she wore them at her cleavage, she showed friendship or remembrance.

Considering not only different meanings for the same flower, but other factors such as the ones mentioned above, it is not difficult to imagine the misunderstandings that inevitably occurred. What fun the young people must have had trying to figure out their tussie-mussies in the privacy of their rooms later that night while referring to their books of flower meanings!

One of the first and lasting ways to interpret flower meanings has been by color: white meant purity or humility, yellow meant cheerfulness (modern) or jealousy (traditional), orange meant creativity or warmth, purple meant royalty or success, red meant love or passion, pink meant friendship, and blue meant calmness or peace.

Today the notion of using flowers to convey meanings continues to bloom. We continue to hang wreaths on our doors for various holidays and seasons with the flowers selected for color and the time of year. Florists encourage patrons to carefully choose flowers according to meanings, especially for weddings, proms and funerals. And how could we forget the meaning of mistletoe hung over a door at Yule time?

Whether consciously or not, we convey meanings through our usages of specific flowers. I hope this book will help you to interpret the associations of flowers that you give and receive.

CORRESPONDENCES (MEANINGS)

Abandonment
Windflower (Anemone), Japanese Anemone, Grape

Abruptness
Borage

Absence
Artemisia, Mugwort, Sagebrush, Wormwood

Absent Friends
Zinnia

Abundance
Azalea, Chrysanthemum (Mum), Corn, Wheat

Accept a Faithful Heart
Weigela

Accept Change
Honesty

Acceptance
Cuckoo, Heather, Lilac

Accomplishment
Laurel

Accommodating Disposition
Valerian

Achievement
Rose (Gold), Ivy

Achievement in the Arts
Laurel

Acknowledgment
Bell Flower, Canterbury Bell, Lavender

Action
Chamomile, Dog Fennel, Marguerite, Mayweed (Mayflower)

Activity
Thyme

Address Rejected
Herb Frost

Admiration
African violet, Amethyst, Browallia, Camellia, Carnation (Red), Carnation (Yellow), Dianthus, Heather, Lavender Heather

Adoration
White Camellia, Dwarf Sunflower, Sunflower

Adroitness
Spider Orchid

Adulation
Indian Plantain

Adversity
Blackthorn

Advice
Rhubarb

Secret Meanings of Flowers

Affection
Cactus, Calendula (Pot Marigold), Celosia, Coxcomb, Gorse,
Ivy, Jonquil, Mistletoe, Morning Glory, Oxalis (Sorrel), Pear,
Pear Tree, Pinks (Dianthus), Saxifrage, Stock, Viola, Violet,
Wormwood, Zinnia (Magenta)

Affection beyond the Grave
Locust Tree

Affection Returned
Jonquil

Affluence
Beech tree, Chestnut tree

Aflame
German Iris

Afterthought
White Aster, Michaelmas Daisy, Starwort

Age
Gueleder Rose, Snowball, Tree of Life

Agitation
Rhododendron, Sainfoin, Quaking Grass, Telegraph Plant

Agreement
Corn Straw, Lancaster Rose, Phlox, Straw Flower, Straw

Airy
Delphinium, Larkspur

Alas my Poor Heart
Red Camellia, Deep Red Carnation

Allure
Fern, Tyme

Alternatives
Scabiosa

Always
Rose

Always Cheerful
Coreopsis

Always Lovely
Tea Rose

Always on My Mind
Pink Carnation

Always Reliable
Cress

Always Remembered
Cotton Weed, Everlasting

Always Yours
Red Salvia

Am I Forgotten?
Holly

Am I Indifferent to You?
Dogwood Tree

Am Not Proud
Petunia

Ambassador of love
Cabbage Rose

Ambition
Hollyhock, Mountain Laurel, Ivy

Ambition of a Hero
Mountain Laurel

Ambition of a Scholar
Hollyhock

(The) Ambition of my Love Plagues Itself
Fuchsia

Amiability
Fuchsia, Jasmine

Among the Noblest
Tulip poplar

Amusement
Bladdernut Tree

Ancestors
Bougainvillea

Anger
Furze, Gorse, Peony, Petunia,

Anger Management
Alyssum

Animosity
Basil, St. John's Wort

Anti-Hunger
Alfalfa

Anti-Lightening
Hazel, Holly, Mahogany

Anti-Theft
Aspen, Caraway, Garlic, Juniper, Larch, Vetivert

Anticipation
Anemone (Wind Flower), Bachelor's Button, Basket Flower, Bluebottle, Centaurea, Cornflower, Gooseberry, Hurtsickle

Antidote
Plumbago

Anxiety Relief
Christmas Rose, Hellebore, Lenten Rose

Anxious and Trembling
Red Columbine

Apology
Purple Hyacinth

Appointed Meeting
Pea

Architecture
Candytuft

Ardent Attachment
Delphinium, Larkspur

Ardent Love
Balsam

Ardent and Pure Love
Impatiens

Ardor
Arum, Bearded Iris, Carnation (Red), Cuckoo Flower, Dragon Root, Fleur-de-Lis, Wake Robin

Argument
Fig

Arrogance
Crown Imperial, Indian Tobacco, Lobelia, Pukeweed, Sunflower

Art and Arts
Acanthus, Clematis, Hoya, Wax Plant

Artifice (Pretense)
Acanthus, Flytrap, Clematis, Sweet William

Arts, The
Acanthus, Alder Tree

Aspiration/Aspiring
Bellflower, Hollyhock, Foxtail Lily

Assignation
Chickweed, Pimpernel

Astonishment
Dragon's Wort

Astral Projection
Belladonna, Dittany of Crete, Mugwort

Asylum
Juniper

Athletic Victory
Woodruff

Atonement
Florists' Nightmare (Ormithogalum), Star of Bethlehem

Attachment
Crocus, Heliotrope, Jasmine, Saffron, Moonflower, Red Morning Glory

Attract Love
Lady's Mantle

Attraction
Buttercup, Gorse

Attractive
Foamflower

Attractive to the Opposite Sex
Lemon verbena

Audacity
Larch Tree

Austerity
Thistle

Avarice
Auricula (Bear's Ears)

Availability
Wild geranium

Secret Meanings of Flowers

Aversion
Pinks

Awe
Pine or Fir Tree

Awareness
St. John's Wort

Baby's Hands
Japanese Maple tree

Balance
Candytuft, Hellebore, Mock orange, Saxifrage, White violet

Banquet
Parsley

Bantering
Southernwood

Baseness
Dodder of Thyme

Bashful Love
Damask Rose

Bashful Shame
Deep Red Rose

Bashfulness
Humble Plant, Mimosa Tree, Peony, Prayer Plant, Sensitive Plant, Shame Plant, Sleeping Grass, Touch-M-Not

Be Cautious
Goldenrod

Be Mine
Four- Leaf Clover

Be my Support
Black Bryony

Be of Good Cheer
Poinsettia

Be Warned in Time
Echites (Devil's Potato)

Beautiful But Timid
Amaryllis

Beautiful Eyes
Variegated Tulip

Beautiful Lady
Orchid

Beautiful Mouth
Eustoma (Lisanthus), Prairie Gentian, Prairie Rose, Texas Bluebell

Beauty
Acacia, Avocado, Calla Lily, Camellia (Red or White), Carnation, Carnation (Pink), Catnip, Cherry Blossom, Cinnamon, Daisy (Gerbera), Daisy (Transvaal), Daisy (White), Flax, Ginseng, Hyacinth (White), Lilac, Lily (White), Magnolia, Maidenhair Fern, Maple Tree, Orchid, Orchid (Chinese Ground), Orchid (Cymbidium), Orchid (Hardy), Rosebud, White Weeping Birch

Beauty Always New
Rose (China)

Beauty in Retirement
Acacia

Beauty Is Your Only Attraction
Japan Rose

Beauty Unknown to Possessor
Red Daisy

Beginnings
Birch Tree, Parsley and Rue together

Belief
Pasqual Flower, Garden anemone

Belle
Orchid

Beloved Child
Cinquefoil

Beneficence
Marsh Mallow, Olive Tree, Potato

Benevolence
Allspice, Bubby Bush (Calycanthus), Carolina Allspice, Flax,
Sweet Betsy, Sweet Shrub

Benevolent Justice
Pear

Best Wishes
Basil

Betrothal
Red carnation

Betrayed / Betrayal
Judas Tree, White Catchfly

Better Things To Come
Apple Blossom

Beware
Begonia, Oleander, Rhododendron, Hensbane

Beware of Excesses
Saffron

Beware of Excess Pleasures
Rue

Beware of the Coquette
Catalpa

Binding
Knotweed

Birth
Dittany of Crete, Lotus, Oregano

Bitter Memories
Pheasant's Eye

Bitter Truth
Nightshade

Bitterness
Aloe, Russian Olive, Wormwood

Blessings of Being Single
Bachelor's Button, Basket Flower, Bluebottle, Cornflower, Hurtsickle

Bliss
Everlasting Pea, Grass Pea, Sweetpea

Blocks Emotional Conflicts
Lavender

Bluntness
Borage

Blushes
Marjoram

Boaster
Hydrangea

Boastfulness
Hydrangea

Boldness
Carnation, Delphinium, Dianthus, Pinks, Larch, Sweet William

Bonds
Bindweed (Convolvulus)

Bonds of Affection
Stock, Dwarf Morning Glory, Gillyflower

Bonds of Love
Honeysuckle, Carnation

Boredom
Guelder Rose, Snowball

Bound
Snowball

Braggart
Hydrangea

Bravery
Cactus, Oak Tree, Oak Leaves, Peony

Breaking Love Spells
Pistachio

Breaking Up
Day Lily, Lily

Breath of an Angel
Moon Vine (Moonflower)

Bridal Festivities
Orange Flower

Brilliant Complexion
Damask Rose

Broken Heart
Yellow Rose

Brouhaha
Rhubarb

Buddhism
Bo Tree

Budding Beauty
Mayflower

Building
Red Clover

Bulk
Gourd, Watermelon

Bullet-proofing
Edelweiss

Bury Me Amid Nature's Beauties
Persimmon

Busybody
Cardinal Vine

Calling Spirits
Dandelion, Wormwood

Calming Thoughts
Skullcap

Calmness
Buck Bean, Lisianthus (Eustoma), Rushes, Bilberry, Love-in-a-mist, Snowflake

Calumny (Slander)
Hellebore, Lenten Rose

Capability
Coneflower

Capricious Beauty
Musk Rose, Lady's slipper

Capriciousness
Dahlia, Lady's Slipper Orchid, Purple Carnation

Cares
Calendula (Pot marigold)

Caring
Pink Tulip

Carousing
Grape

Cat Magic
Catnip

Catch Me if You Can
Lady Slipper Orchid

Caught/Caught At Last
Venus Flytrap

Caution
Azalea, Oleander

Celebration
Bramble, Poinsettia

Celibacy
Bachelor's Button, Basket Flower, Bluebottle, Centaurea,
Cornflower, Hurtsickle

Challenge
Alum Root, Coral Bells

Character
Gladiolus

Chagrin
Marigold

Challenge
Coral bells, Holly

Change
Ash Tree, Birch Tree, Pimpernel

Changeable Disposition
Rye Grass

Charity
Wild Grape, Nasturtium, Turnip

Charm
Diosma (Breath of Heaven), Buttercup, Lily

Charming
Aster

Chaste Love
Acacia

Chastity
Cucumber, Everlasting Pea, Hawthorn, Lavender, Orange
Flower, Cactus, Camphor, Coconut, Cucumber, Fleabane,

Hemlock, Lettuce, Pineapple, Sweet Pea, Vervain, Witch Hazel

Cheer Up
Eyebright

Cheerful/Cheerfulness
Yellow Carnation, Coreopsis, Tickseed, Chrysanthemum (Mum), Crocus, Daisy, Saffron, Buttercup, Yellow Chrysanthemum, English daisy

Cheerfulness in Old Age
Chrysanthemum (Mum), Starwort

Cheerfulness In Adversity
Chinese Chrysanthemum, Everlasting

Cheers My Soul
Quince

Cheers the Heart
Bugle (Ajuga)

Cherished
Meadow Sage, Salvia

Childhood
Sweet William

Childishness
Buttercup (Narcissus), Geranium

Chivalry
Buttercup, Carnation, Cherry, Daffodil, Dianthus (Pinks, Sweet William), Jonquil, Monkshood, Wolfbane

Chosen One
Pimpernel

Christmas Joy
Holly berries

Civil Service
Laurel

Clarity
Bilberry

Clarity of Thoughts
Pennyroyal

Cleanliness
Hyssop

Cleansing
Nicotiana, Camphor

Cleverness
Saxifrage, Strawberry begonia

Coarseness (Vulgarity)
Pumpkin

Cold-Hearted
Lettuce

Coldness
Fig Marigold, Chaste bush

Color Of My Fate
Coral Honeysuckle

Come Down
Jacob's Ladder

Comfort / Comforting
Pear Tree, Scarlet Geranium, Chamomile, Geranium, Ginger, Tea

Comfort to those who Mourn
Sage

Come to Me
Balsam, Bridal Wreath (Stephanotis)

Comeliness
Cowslip, Primrose

Coming of Age
Mayflower

Communication
Bilberry, Mullein, Scabiosa

Communication with the Spirit/Spirits
Staghorn Sumac

Compassion
Allspice, Elder Tree, Bee balm (Monarda), Elderberry, Passionflower

Compliance
Reeds

Concealed Love
Acacia, Almond Tree, Motherwort

Concealed Merit
Coriander

Conceit/Conceited
Cockscomb, Spirea, Pomegranate

Conception
Mugwort

Concert
Nettle

Concord
Apple

Confessed Love/Confession of Love
Moss Rosebud

Confidence
Bird's Nest Fern, Coxcomb, Fern, Hepatica, Liverwort

Confiding Love
Fuchsia

Conflict
Blackthorn

Congeniality
Jasmine

Conjugal Affection
Ivy, Linden Tree, Lime Tree, Geranium

Conquest
Nasturtium

Consistency
Baby's Breath, Bluebell, Dogwood Tree, Forget-Me-Not,
Globe Amaranth, Hyacinth, Scarlet Zinnia

Consolation
Snowdrop, Red Poppy

Constancy in Friendship
Boxwood

Constancy
Cedar Tree, Bellflower, Blue Hyacinth, Box, Bluebell,
Canterbury Bells, Hyacinth, Marigold, Wild geranium, Ivy

Consumed By Love
Althea, Mallow, Rose of Sharon

Content
Houstonia

Contempt
Carnation (Yellow), Rue

Contentment
Aster, Bluet, Houstonia, Camelia

Contrition
Peony

Coquetry
Damask Violet, Gillyflower, Dame's Rocket, Lily, Mother of
the Evening, Summer Lilac, Sweet Rocket, Dandelion, Day
Lily, Morning Glory

Cordiality
Peppermint, Woodruff

Could You Bear Poverty?
Browallia

Counterfeit
Mock Orange

Courage
Abyssinian, Aspen, Black Cohosh, Black Poplar Tree, Borage, Chives, Columbine, Edelweiss, Everlasting Pea, Fennel, Garlic, Laurel, Master Wort, Mullein, Pine Tree, Poke, Ragweed, Sweet Pea, Sword Lily, Tea, Thyme, Yarrow

Courtliness
Cranesbill, Geranium

Courtship
Healther

Creation of Beauty
Laurel

Creative Force
Red and white rose

Creativity
Alder Tree, Clematis, Pentsemon, Basil, Elecampane, Mock orange

Crime
Tamarisk

Criticism
Cucumber

Cruelty In Love
Marigold, Nettle

Cure
Balm of Gilead

Cure For Heartache
Yarrow, Cranberry

Curiosity
Asparagus Fern, Sycamore Tree

Daintiness
Aster, Cornflower, Sweet Sultan

Dainty Pleasures
Coral bells

Dance with Me
Magic Lily (Lycoris), Maltese Cross, Naked Lady, Ragged Robin, Spider Lily

Danger / Dangerous
Rhododendron, Red Hot Poker, Torch Lily, Tuberose, Henbit

Dangerous Pride
Blackberry

Daring
Pine Tree

Dark Thoughts
Begonia, Nightshade

Daughter's Sweetness
Wisteria

Dauntlessness
Statice

Dead Hope
Morning Glory

Deadly Foe Is Near
Monkshood

Death
Poppy, Black Rose, Cypress Tree

Death Is Preferable to Loss of Innocence
Dried White Rose

Deceit
Angel's Trumpet, Cypress Tree, Datura, Devil's Cucumber,
Devil's Trumpet, Geranium, Jimson Weed Mock Orange,
Prickly Burr, Thorn Apple, Venus Flytrap

Deceitful Charms
Datura, Thorn Apple

Deception
Cherry Tree, Dogbane, Linaria, Monkshood, Snapdragon,
Toad Flax

Decisions
Foxglove

Declaration of Love
Red Tulip

Decreased Love
Yellow Rose

Dedication
Hyacinth

Deep, Pure Love
Red carnation

Deep Romance
Red Canterbury Bells

Deep Thoughts
Begonia

Defense
Holly, Rowan Tree

Dejection
Aloe, Chrysanthemum (Yellow), Lichen, Lupine

Delay
Ageratum, Joe Pye Weed, White Snakeroot

Delicacy/Delicate
Bachelor's Button, Centaurea, Love in a Mist (Nigella),
Bottlebrush, Century Plant, Cornflower, St. Bridgid de Caen
(Anemone), Sweet Sultan, Dusty Miller

Delicate Beauty
Flower of an Hour, Hibiscus, Malva, Mallow, Hibiscus,
Muskmallow, Orchid, Rose Mallow, Rose of Sharon

Delicate Love Connection
African Violet

Delight/Delightful
Caladium, Cineraria

Delusion
Marjoram

Democracy
White Carnation

Departure
Everlasting Pea, Grass Pea, Morning Glory, Sweet Pea, Pea

Desertion/Forsaken
Columbine, Anemone, Windflower

Desire
Cactus, Hawthorn Tree, Jonquil, Rose (Coral, Orange, Peach)

Desire for Riches
Buttercup, Kingscup

Desire to Please
Mezereon, Daphne Odora

Desire to Travel
Bridal Wreath

Desolate Heart
Chrysanthemum (Mum)

Despair
Cypress Tree, Marigold

Despair Not
White Julienne

Despondency
Convolvulus (Bindweed, Morning Glory), Marigold

Destiny
Ash Tree

Determined / Determination
Red Hot Poker, Torch Lily, Canary Grass

Devoted Love / Devoted Affection
Honeysuckle

Devotion
White Carnation, Dianthus, Heliotrope, Lavender, Sunflower, Hosta, Hydrangea

Dexterity
Sweet William

Difficulty/Difficulties
Blackthorn

Diffidence
Cyclamen, Persian Violet

Dignity
Apple of Peru, Ash Tree, Cloves, Dahlia, Elm Tree, Magnolia Tree, Shoo Fly Plant, Artemisia

Diligence
Red Clover

Directness
Borage

Disappointed Expectation
Fish Geranium

Disappointed in Love
Weeping Willow

Disappointment
Yellow Carnation Carolina Syringa (Lilac)

Discipline
Bayberry, Wax Myrtle

Discretion
Maidenhair Fern, Lemon Blossom, Lemon

Disdain
Yellow Carnation, Rue

Disguise
Thorn Apple

Disgust
Frog Lily, Fungus

Dislike
Tansy

Disquietude
Pot Marigold

Distaste
Yellow Dahlia

Distinction
Cardinal Flower, Lobelia

Distrust
Lavender

Diversity
Aster

Divination
Dittany of Crete, Broom, Camphor, Cherry, Corn, Dandelion, Dodder, Dogbane, Fig, Goldenrod, Ground Ivy, Hibiscus, Lettuce, Meadowsweet, Mullein, Orange, Orris, Pansy, Pomegranate, Roots, Rose, Rue, St. John's Wort, Willow

Divine Beauty
Cowslip, Primrose (Primula)

Divine Guidance
Goldenrod

Divinity/Divine
Cowslip, Primrose

Do Me Justice
Chestnut Tree

Do Not Abuse
Saffron

Do Not Forget Me
Forget-Me-Not, Mouse Ear

Do Not Hurt Me
Mimosa

Do Not Refuse Me
California Poppy, Queen Anne's Lace

Do Not Stand Still
Kudzu

Do You Love Me?
Honeysuckle

Do You Still Love Me?
Lilac

Docility
Bulrush, Rushes

Domestic Duties
Meadow Sage, Sage

Domestic Happiness
Flax, Grape, Holly, Honeysuckle, Sage

Domestic Industry
Houseleek

Domestic Virtue
Sage

Dormant Affection
White Poppy

Doubt/Distrust
Apricot

Drama
Amaryllis, Belladonna Lily, Naked Lady

Dread
Dragon Plant

Dream Magic
Holly, Huckleberry

Dreaminess
Poppy, Pink Tulip

Dreams
Forget-Me-Not, Gentian, Huckleberry, Pimpernel, Texas
Mountain Laurel

Dreams of Fantasy
Mauve Carnation

Drunk and Blousy
Valerian

Drunkenness
Vine

Durability
Cornet, Dogbane

Duration
Cherry Tree

Dying Love
Yellow Rose

Eagerness
Heliotrope

Early Attachment
Thornless Rose, Blue Periwinkle

Early Friendship
Blue Periwinkle, Vinca

Ease
Gooseberry

Eases Cares and Worries
Stitchwort

Economy
Chicory

Ecstasy
Gardenia

Education
Cherry Blossom, Flowering Cherry Tree, Clover, Celandine

Egotism
Daffodil, Narcissus

Elation
Pine or Fir Tree

Elegance
Acacia (Rose or White), Birch Tree, Bleeding Heart, Carolina
Jasmine, Cranesbill, Dahlia, Diosma, Dutchman's Britches,
Geranium, Hearts (White), Jasmine, Jasmine (Yellow), Lily,
Locust Tree, Maple Tree, Monk's Head, Pomegranate
Flower, Soldier's Cap, Squirrel Corn

Elevation
Fir Trees

Elope with Me/ Elopement
Basket Lily, Cleome, Ismene, Peruvian Daffodil, Sea Daffodil, Spider Lily, Spider Flower, Scorpion Orchid

Eloquence
Apostle Plant, Flags, Iris, Walking Iris, White Water Lily, Cape Myrtle, Lotus, Aspin, Fleur de Lis, Mexican Sage

Embarrassment
Love-In-A-Puzzle, Love in a Mist, Nigella

Eminence
Bindweed

Emotion
Willow Tree

Emotional Balance
Chamomile

Emotional Calmness
Nettle

Emotional Stability
Elecampane

Emotions
Rue

Employment
Devil's Shoestring, Lucky Hand, Pecan Tree

Enchantment
Lavender Rose, Verbena, Vervain, Holly

Encouragement
Artemisia, Black-Eyed Susan, Carnation (Pink), Galax
Goldenrod, Mugwort, Sagebrush, Wandflower, Wormwood

Endearing Affection
Gorse

Endearment
White Carnation

Ending Relationships
Turnip

Endings
Cyclamen, Yew

Endurance
Cactus, Dock, Oak Tree, Pine

Enduring Beauty
Gillyflower, Queen Anne's Thimbles

Enemy
Orange Lily

Energy
Chamomile, Columbine, Dog Fennel, Marguerite, Mayweed,
Thyme, Dandelion, Gooseberry, Red Salvia, Snapdragon

Energy in Adversity
Chamomile

Engagement
Grape Hyacinth

Enjoyment
Double Daisy, Gooseberry

Enlightenment
Hazel, Lotus

Ennui
Guelder Rose, Snowball, Moss

Entertainment
Parsley

Enthusiasm
Blazing Star, Bouvardia, Coral Rose, Day Lily, Elecampaine,
Gay Feather, Kansas Feather, Orange Rose, Peach Rose, Pine
or Fir Tree, Scabiosa, Snakeroot

Envy
Bramble, Briars, Crane's Bill, Crow's Bill, Wild Geranium

Error
Orchid

Escape
Celandine

Esteem
Daffodil, Geranium, Meadow Sage, Sage, Pineapple Sage

Esteem, but Not Love
Spiderwort

Estranged Love
Anemone, Lotus

Eternal Love
Heliotrope, Orange Blossom, White Rose

Eternal Sleep
Poppy

Eternal Youth
Fern

Eternity
Everlasting

Evanescent Pleasure
Poppy

Evening
Damask Violet, Dame's Gillyflower, Dame's Rocket, Dame's
Violet, Lilac, Mother of the Evening, Night-Scented
Gillyflower, Sweet Rocket

Everlasting Friendship
Arborvitae

Excellence
Camellia

Excellence beyond Beauty
Alyssum, Aurinia

Excess Is Dangerous
Saffron

Excess of Sensibility
Aspen Tree

Excitement
Bronze Chrysanthemum (Mum), Red and Yellow Rose together

Expectancy/Expectation
Gooseberry, Anemone, Hawthorn Tree, Zephyr Flower

Expected Meeting
Nutmeg Geranium

Extent
Gourd

Extinguished Hopes
Convolvulus Major (Morning Glory)

Extravagance
Poppy

Extinguished Hopes
Bindweed, Morning Glory

Extreme Betrayal
Rose (Yellow)

Exuberance
Crocus

Facility
Valerian, Apple Geranium, Speedwell

Fading Love
Anemone

Failure
Lavender

Fairies' Fire
Pyrus Japonica

Faith
Anemone, Apostle Plant, Compass Flower, Dogwood Tree, Iris (Flags), Passion Flower, Walking Iris, Violet

Faithful
Croton

Faithful Heart
Frankincense

Faithful In Misfortune
Wall Flower

Faithful Love
Ageratum, Coxcomb

Faithfulness
African Violet, Arbutus, Bird of Paradise, Bluebell, Carnation, Crane Flower, Dahlia, Daisy, Dandelion, Dianthus, Gillyflower, Heliotrope, Lemon Blossom, Madrone Tree, Strawberry, Blue Violet, Dogwood Tree, Verbena

Faithfulness in Adversity
Wallflower

Falsehood
Bugloss, Dogbane, Yellow Lily, Nightshade

False Love
White Rose

Fame
Apple Tree, Apple Blossom, Begonia, Climbing Lily,
Creeping Lily, Daphne, Fire Lily, Flame Lily, Glory Lily,
Tulip, Tulip Poplar Tree

Fame Speaks Well Of Him
Apple

Family Union
Pink Verbena

Fanciful
Rose Lupine

Farsightedness
Holly

Farewell
Cyclamen, Michaelmas Daisy, Spruce Tree, Black Rose

Fascination
Canterbury Bells, Carnation, Carnation (Red), Carnation
(Yellow), Dianthus, Fern, Fern (Boston), Honesty, Money
Plant, Nightshade, Rose (Orange)

Fashion/Fashionable
Queen's Rocket

Fastidiousness
Lilac

Fate
Ash Tree, Flax, Hemp

Fault
Henbit

Favors
Chicory

Fealty
Ivy

Fear
Aspen Tree, Hawthorn Tree

Feasting
Parsley

Fecundity (Fruitfulness)
Fig, Hollyhock

Felicity
Balsam, Cornflower, Dusty Miller, Impatiens, Sweet Sultan

Fellowship
Balm, Melissa

Female Ambition
Hollyhock (White)

Female Attraction
Henbit (Henbane)

Female Fidelity
Speedwell, Veronica

Feminine Charm
Gardenia

Feminine Modesty
Calla Lily

Femininity
Aster, Azalea, Queen Anne's Lace

Ferocity
Arum

Fertility
Agaric, Banana, Bistort, Carrot, Chaste Tree, Cucumber,
Cyclamen, Hollyhock, Lotus, Orange Blossom, Palm, Persian
Violet, Bodhi, Chickweed, Cuckoo Flower, Daffodil, Date,
Dock, Fig, Geranium, Grape, Hawthorn, Hazel, Horsetail,
Mandrake, Mistletoe, Mustard, Nuts, Olive, Patchouli, Peach,
Pinecone, Pine Tree, Pomegranate, Poppy, Rice, Sunflower,
Verbena, Wheat

Festivity
Baby's Breath, Parsley

Fickleness
Abatina, Delphinium, Larkspur, Larkspur (Pink),Lady's
Slipper

Fidelity
Aster, Bleeding Heart, Bluebell, Chili Pepper, Clover
Dutchman's Britches, Hearts (White), Honeysuckle, Ivy,
Lemon Blossom, Licorice, Magnolia Tree, Rhubarb,
Rosemary, Rye Skullcap, Vetch

Fidelity in Love
Lemon

Filial Love
Clematis

Finding Other Ways Of Doing Things
Scabiosa

Finding Your Way
Daisy

Fine Arts
Acanthus

Finesse
Carnation, Dianthus, Pinks, Sweet William

Fire
Fraxinella, Horehound

Fiery Love
Rose of Sharon (Althea)

First Love
Lilac, Lilac, (Purple, Lily (Purple)

Fishing Magic
Cotton, Hawthorn

Fitness
Flag

Flame
Camellia (Red), Iris

Flashy
Carnation (Red)

Flattery
Venus' Looking Glass

Flattery and Deceit
Fennel

Flee Away
Pennyroyal

Fleeting Life/Growing Older
Grass

Flexibility
Honesty

Flights of Fancy
Delphinium, Larkspur

Flirtation/Flirting/Flirt
Dandelion, Day Lily, Feverfew, Lily (Yellow), Mezereon

Flower of the Gladiators
Gladiolus (Glads), Sword Lily

Flying
Basil, Poplar Tree

Foe Is Near
Monkshood

Folly
Columbine, Cranesbill, Geranium

Fond Caresses
Fairy Lily, Rain Lily, Zephyr

Foolishness
Columbine

Foppery
Amaranth, Coxcomb

For Once May Pride Befriend Me
Tiger Flower

Forbearance
Azalea

Force
Fennel

Foresight
Crocus, Holly, Saffron, Strawberry

Forever Thine
Dahlia, Salvia (Red)

Forgetfulness
Honesty, Money Plant, Moonwort

Forget-Me-Not
Mouse Ear, Myosotis (Forget-Me-Not), Pansy (Purple and Yellow), Scorpion Grass

Forgive and Forget
Rose (Yellow)

Forgiveness
Asphodel, Creeping Jennie, Gooseneck Loosestrife

Forgiveness of Injuries
Cinnamon

Formality
Narcissus

Forsaken
Anemone, Weeping Willow Tree

Forgetfulness
Moonwort

Fortitude
Chamomile

Fortune
Peruvian Lily

Fragile
Anemone, Azalea

Fragile Passion
Azalea

Fragrance Remembered
Tussie Mussie

Frankness
Osier

Fraternal Affection
Honeysuckle, Lilac, Woodbine

Fraternal Regard
Lilac

Freedom
Water Willow, Willow Tree

Friendliness
Wheat

Friendship
Acacia, Apostle Plant, Carnation (Pink), Chrysanthemum, Cranesbill, Freesia, Galax, Geranium, Gerbera Daisy, Lemon, Love Seed, Lucky Seed, Passion Flower, Peruvian Lily, Pussy Willow, Rose (Light Pink), Sweet Pea, Walking Iris, Wandflower, Wheat, Willow Tree, Zinnia

Friendship in Adversity
Wallflower, Snowdrop

Frigidity
Chicory, Hydrangea

Frivolity
Bladder Nut Tree

Frugality
Chicory, Endive, Fuchsia, Nightshade

Fruitfulness
Hollyhock

Frugality
Chicory, Fuchsia

Fulfillment
Raspberry

Fun
Delphinium, Larkspur, Lemon Balm, Pansy, Tiger Lily

Funerals
Hawthorn

Future
Apple Blossom

Future Joy
Celandine, Figwort, Pilewort

Future Promise
Strawberry

Gaiety
Baby's Breath, Delphinium, Larkspur, Lily (Yellow)

Gallantry
Carnation, Daffodil (Yellow), Dianthus (Pinks, Sweet William), Nosegay

Gambling
Devil's Shoestring

Games
Hyacinth

Garden Magic
Apple, Grape

General Love
Furze

Generosity
Calycanthus (Bubby Bush, Carolina Allspice, Sweet Shrub),
Gladiolus, Globe Flower, Honeysuckle, Orange

Generous and Devoted Love (Affection)
Honeysuckle

Genius
Eglantine, Plum Tree, Sycamore Tree

Gentle- Heartedness
Raspberry

Gentleness
Lamb's Ears, Provence Rose

Gentility
Cockle, Cranesbill, Geranium

Giddiness
Almond

Gift of Mother Nature
Corn

Gifts of the Holy Spirit
Columbine

Gift to a Man
Camellia

Girlhood
Rose (Short-stemmed), Rosebud (White)

Give an Account of Yourself
Chickweed

Give Me a Break
Gladiolus

Give Me Your Good Wishes
Basil

Gladness
Cicely, Crocus, Myrrh, Rose, Saffron, Tea

Glorious Beauty
Morning Glory

Glory
Bay Tree, Bloodbloom, Blood Flower, Blood Lily, Cape Lily, Cape Tulip, Catherine Wheel, Daphne, Fireball Lily, Laurel, Poison Root

Go
Rue

Goals
Oriental Hellebore, Wild Violet

Go Not Away
Sweet Pea

Good Cheer
Poinsettia

Good Education
Cherry Tree

Good Fortune
Goldenrod

Good Government
Pear

Good Health
Feverfew

Good Luck
Aloe, Bayberry, Bells of Ireland, Clover, Garlic, Job's Tears, Mugwort, Stephanotis, White Heather

Good Luck in the New Year
Rosemary

Good Natured
Forsythia, Mullein

Good News
Guelder Rose

Good Perspective
Bird of Paradise

Good Taste
Dahlia, Fuchsia

Good Wishes
Holly

Good Works
Cherry

Good-bye
Cyclamen, Persian Violet, Sweet Pea

Goodness
Goosefoot, Strawberry, White Zinnia

Goodwill
Holly

Gossip
Cobaea, Canterbury Bells, Cup and Saucer
Gossip Stopper
Slippery Elm

Grace
Acacia (Pink), Asparagus Fern, Aster, Bamboo, Birch Tree, Cowslip, Jasmine, Jasmine (Yellow), Primrose, Rose (Multiflora)

Gracefulness
Carolina Jasmine, White Geranium

Graciousness
Camellia, Flamingo Flower, Painter's Palette, Snapdragon

Grandeur
Ash Tree, Cactus

Grant Me a Smile
Dianthus (Carnation, Pinks, Sweet William)

Gratitude
Agrimony, Bell Flower, Bluebell, , Bouquet of Roses, Camellia, Canterbury Bells, Carnation (Pink), Dahlia, Globeflower, Parsley, Purple Sage, Statice

Gratitude to Parents
Dahlia (White)

Great Beauty
Canna Lily

Great Joy
Caladium

Grief
Aloe, Bell Flower, Harebell, Hyacinth (Purple), Marigold, Thistle

Grounding
Cuckoo Flower

Growing Indifference
Water Lily (Yellow)

Growing Old
Meadow Saffron

Growth
Ash Tree, Ivy

Guidance
Alser Tree

Hands Full of Cash
Peony

Happiness
Adam and Eve Roots, Artemisia, Baby's Breath, Catnip,
Celandine, Coreopsis, Cumin, Cyclamen, Dandelion, Dusty
Miller,
Hawthorn Tree, Honeysuckle, High John The Conqueror,
Hyacinth, Lavender, Lily (Yellow), Lily of the Valley, ,
Marjoram, Meadowsweet, Mugwort, Peony, Purslane,
Quince, Raspberry, Rose, St. John's Wort, Saffron,
Sagebrush, Sunflower, Tickseed, , Wormwood

Happiness in Marriage
Bridal Wreath, Pea

Happy Always
Lupine (White)

Happy Love
Bridal Rose

Happy Thoughts
Johnny Jump Up

Happy Years
Tulip

Hard Work
Clover, Coral Bells

Hardness
Cranberry, Fennel

Harmony
Pimpernel

Harshness
Thistle

Hatred
Basil, Fumitory, Lily (Orange), Rose (Black)

Haughtiness
Amaryllis, Delphinium, Sunflower (Tall)

Have Pity On My Passion
Jonquil

Head over Heels
Vine

Healing
Achillea, Aloe, Althea, Apple, Basil, Black Sampson, Broom, Butterfly Bush, Columbine, Coneflower, Cowslip, Cucumber, Fern, Flax, Garlic, Marshmallow, Mignonette, Peony, Primrose, Rue, Sacred Plant, Yarrow, Adder's Tongue, Allspice, Amaranth, Angelica, Balm of Gilead, Lemon Balm, Barley, Bay, Bittersweet, Blackberry, Bracken, Carnation, Cedar Tree, Cinnamon, Citron, Coriander, Cotton, Cowslip, Cucumber, Cypress Tree, Dock Eucalyptus, Fennel, Gardenia, Ginseng, Goat's Rue, Golden Seal, Heliotrope, Hemp, Henna, Hops, Horehound, Horse Chestnut, Ivy, Job's Tears, Mesquite, Mint, Mugwort, Myrrh, Nettle, Onion, Pepper Tree, Peppermint, Persimmon, Pine, Plantain, Plum, Potato, Rose, Rosemary, Rowan Tree, Saffron, Sandalwood,

Wood Sorrel, Spearmint, Thistle, Thyme, Tobacco, Vervain, Violet, Willow, Wintergreen

Healing and Charm
Digitalis

Healing of the Spirit
Gentian

Healing Properties
Bachelor's Button

Heals Conflicts
Currant

Heals Indifference
Scabiosa

Health
Anemone, Apple, Ash Tree, Camphor, Caraway, Carob, Coriander, Fern, Figwort, Geranium, Ginger (Blue), Goat's Rue, Gorse, Iceland Moss,, Juniper, Knotweed, Larkspur, Marigold, Marjoram, Mandrake, Mistletoe, Mullein, Pear Tree, Pimpernel, Rue, Sassafras, St. John's Wort, Sunflower, Tansy, Thyme, Walnut

Health and Energy
Carnation (Mixed Colors)

Heart
Anthurium

Heart Innocent of Love
Rosebud

Heart Is Agitated
Hazel

Heartache Ease
Achillea, Butterfly Weed, Yarrow

Heart's Comfort
Marigold

Heart's Mystery
Polyanthus, Primrose

Heartlessness
Amaranthus, Hydrangea, Love Lies Bleeding

Heaven
Coleus, Snowball

Heavenly
Rose (White)

Heedlessness
Almond

Help Against Wearisomeness
Chamomile

Helpfulness
Black Bryony, Juniper Tree, Lady's Seal

Helpless and Delicate
Wisteria

Hermitage
Milkwort

Hex Breaking
Toadflax

Hidden Love
Acacia

Hidden Worth
Cilantro (Coriander)

High of Soul
Scarlet Lily

Higher Learning
Scabiosa

Holiness
Bramble, Fir Tree, Mistletoe

Holy Wishes
Plumbago

Homage
Sunflower

Home Sweet Home
Comfrey

Honesty
Althea, Marshmallow, Balloon Flower, Chinese Bellflower, Honesty, Money Plant, Verbena (White)

Honor
Cardinal Flower, Climbing Lily, Creeping Lily, Fire Lily, Flame Lily, Lily, Lobelia (Scarlet)

Honoring the Dead
Umbrella Pine Tree

Hope
Almond, Apostle Plant, Apple Blossom, Iris, Florist's Nightmare, Forget-Me-Not, Hawthorn, Pine, Pretty Face, Snowdrop, Star of Bethlehem, Starflower, Walking Iris, Wild Hyacinth

Hope in Adversity
Spruce Tree

Hope in Love
Bachelor's Button, Tulip (Yellow)

Hopeless Love
Yellow Tulip

Hopelessness
Amaranthus, Fountain Plant, Joseph's Coat, Love Lies Bleeding, Prince of Wales Feather, Tampala

Hopeless Not Heartless
Love Lies Bleeding

Horror
Dragonwort, Mandrake

Hospitality
Oak Tree, Oak Sprig, Pineapple, Pineapple Sage, Starwort

Humble Love
Fuchsia

Humiliation
Elder Tree

Humility
Allium, Bellflower, Bindweed, Bluebell, Broomn, Canterbury Gells, Lilac (Field), Lily of the Valley, Woodruff (Blue)

Humor
Celosia, Delphinium, Larkspur, Marjoram

Hunting
Parosela, Primrose (Yellow)

Hypocrisy
Foxglove

I Adore You
Heliotrope

I Am Deeply In Love
Althea

I Am Dazzled By Your Charms
Buttercup, Ranunculus

I Am Happy That You Love Me
Dahlia (Yellow)

I Am Still Available
Carnation (White)

I Am Worthy of You
Rose (White)

I Am Your Captive
Peach

I Await Your Pleasures
Orchid

I Believe in Your Constancy
Boxwood

I Blush for You
Kiss Me Over The Garden Gate, Lady's Thumb, Prince's
Feather (Plume)

I Burn for You
Prickly Pear

I Burn
German Iris

I Cannot Give Thee Up
Columbine

I Change but in Death
Bay Leaf

I Cling To You
Chickweed, Vetch, Virginia Creeper, Wisteria

I Dare You to Love Me
Tiger Lily

I Declare War Against You
Belvedere, Tansy

I Desire a Return Of Affection
Jonquil

I Desire To Please
Wild Geranium

I Die If Neglected
Lauresina, Viburnum

I Do Not Believe You
Carnation (Yellow)

I Doubt You
Dogbane

I Dream of Thee
Osmunda

I Fall into a Trap Laid for Me
Red Catchfly

I Feel Your Kindness
Flax

I Have Cause
Marigold

I Have Lost All
Pincushion Flower, Scabiosa

Secret Meanings of Flowers

I Keep My Secret
Fig

I Like You Only as a Friend
Lavender

I Live but for Thee
Cedar Tree, Mignonette

I Love You
Bloom (Red), Chrysanthemum (Red), Morning Glory, Rose, Rose (Single)

I Love You in Secret
Gardenia

I Love You, Too
Chrysanthemum (Red)

I Love Your Mind
Clematis

I Mourn Your Absence
Zinnia

I'll Never Change
Arborvitae

I Only Dream of Love
Moonflower (Moon Vine)

I Oppose You
Tansy

I Prefer You
Cranesbill, Geranium

I Promise
Clover (White)

I Seek Glory
Hollyhock

I Share Your Sentiments
Aster (Double), English Daisy, Garden Daisy

I Still Love You
Rose (Single)

I Think of Thee
Everlasting, Salvia (Blue)

I Think of You Constantly
Dahlia (Variegated)

I Understand You
Cyclamen

I Will Not Economize
Cyclamen (Red)

I Will Remember You Always / I Will Never Forget You
Carnation (Pink), Rose (Long-stemmed)

I Will Return
Queen Anne's Lace

I Will Still Be Waiting
Astilbe

I Will Think About It
Aster (Single), Daisy, Daisy Wreath

I Will Think of You
China Aster

I Wish I Was Rich
Kingscup

I Will Always Remember
Tea Rose

I Wound To Heal
Eglantine

Idleness
Florist's Nightmare, Star of Bethlehem

If You Love Me, You Will Find It Out
Maiden's Blush, Rose

I'll Pray for You
Hyacinth (White)

I'll Still Be Waiting
Astilbe, False Goat's Beard, False Spirea

I'll Try Again
Blazing Star, Button, Gay Feather, Kansas Feather
Snake Root

Ill-Natured Beauty
Citron

I'm Not Sure You've Been Faithful
Aster

I'm Really Sincere
Gladiolus (Glads), Sword Lily

I'm Sorry
Purple Hyacinth

I Weep for You
Verbena (Purple)

I Will Think About It
Wild Daisy

Illusion
Marjoram

Image Magic
Bryony, Potato, Straw

Imagination
Bluebonnet, Lupine, Poppy, Snowdrop, White Violet

Immortality
Apple, Everlasting, Globe Amaranth, Sage

Immortal Love
Globe Amaranth

Immutability
Yew

Impartiality
Gloriosa Daisy, Rudbeckia (Black-Eyed Susan)

Immunity
Coneflower

Impartiality
Brown-Eyed Susan

Impatience
Balsam, Busy Lizzie, Impatiens, Jewel Weed, Our Lady's Earrings, Patient Lucy, Policeman's Helmet, Sultana, Touch-Me-Not

Impatient of Absence
Corchorus

Importunity
Burdock

Imprudence
Almond, Reed, Plum Tree, White Oak

Impulsiveness
Hyacinth

In My Thoughts
Johnny Jump Up

Inconstancy
Columbine, Evening Primrose, Honeysuckle

Incorruptible
Cedar of Lebanon

Indecision
Carnation (Striped)

Independence
Bachelor's Button, Basket Flower, Bluebottle, Boutonniere Flower, Cornflower, Hurtsickle, Love In A Mist, Thistle

Indifference / Indifferent
Candytuft, Chaste Bush, Dogwood Tree, Mustard, Mustard Seed

Indigence
Evergreen Tree or Shrub

Indignation
Peony

Indiscretion
Almond, Bellflower, Bulrush, Canterbury Bells

Industrious / Industry
Bumblebee Orchid, Clover, Dried Flax, Dusty Miller, Red Clover

Infatuation
Dwarf Sunflower

Infertility
Walnut

Infidelity
Rose (Yellow)

Infidelity Prevented
Caraway

Ingenuity
Clematis, Cranesbill, Geranium, Penciled Geranium

Ingenuous Simplicity
Chickweed

Secret Meanings of Flowers

Ingratitude
Buttercup, Crow's Foot, Gentian (Yellow)

Injustice
Hops

Innate Warmth
Camellia (Red)

Inner Beauty
Delphinium, Larkspur

Inner Power
Dracaena

Inner Self
Daffodil

Inner Wisdom
Sage

Innocence
Acacia, African Daisy, Baby's Breath, White Carnation, Chrysanthemum, Daisy, English Daisy, Freesia, Gerbera Daisy, Lily, Orange Blossom, Rose (White), Violet (White)

Inquietude/Restless
Marigold

Insight
Snowdrop

Insincerity
Cherry, Foxglove, Morning Glory

Insinuation
Bindweed

Inspiration
Alder Tree, Alder Tree, Angelica, Apostle Plant, Bindweed, Columbine, Hazel, Iris, Walking Iris

Instability
Dahlia, Moonflower

Instruction
Bayberry, Wax Myrtle

Integrity
Aloe, Gentian

Intellect
Daisy

Intellectual Excellence
Sumac, Walnut **Tree**

Intelligence
Clematis, Walnut Tree

Intense Emotion
Rose (Yellow)

Intoxicated with Joy
Heliotrope

Intoxication
Grape

Intuition
Pansy, Willow Tree

Invincibility
Aaron's Beard

Invisibility
Amaranth, Chicory, Edelweiss, Heliotrope, Poppy, Wolf's Bane

Ire
Gorse

Irony
Sardony

Irritability
Crabapple Blossom

It's Time
Portulaca

Jealous / Jealousy
Adder's Tongue, Hyacinth (Purple), Hyacinth (Yellow), Marigold, French Marigold, Rose (Yellow)

Joke
Balm, Melissa

Jovial / Joviality
Chrysanthemum, Crocus, Saffron

Joy
Blanket Flower, Burnet, Calendula, Chrysanthemum, Coreopsis, Crocus, Currant, Gaillardia, Gardenia, Hyacinth (Red or Pink), Myrtle, Oxalis, Painted Daisy, Parsley, Pot Marigold, Rose (Red and White), Rose (Yellow), Shamrock, Sorrel, Stitchwort, Tickseed, , Tulip (Yellow), Umbrella Pine Tree, Wood Sorrel

Joys to Come
Celandine

Judgments
Linden Ttee

Justice
Coltsfoot, Rudbeckia, Back-Eyed Susan

Justice Shall Be Done
Coltsfoot, Sweet-Scented Tussilage

Keys
Maple Tree

Kindness
Bluebell, Cherry Blossom, Elderberry

Kiss Me
Mistletoe

Kiss Me Twice before I Rise
Love In A Mist, Nigella

Kiss Me Across The Garden Gate
Kiss me across the garden gate (Polygonum orientale)

Knot Magic
Dodder

Knowledge
Hazel

Lamentation / Sighing
Aspen Tree, Aspen Leaf

Lasting Affection
Zinnia (Magenta)

Lasting Beauty
Gillyflower, Stock

Laugh At Trouble
Harlequin Flower, Wandflower

Learning
Cherry Blossom

Let Me Go
Blood Flower, Butterfly Weed, Red Swallowwort

Let Me Love You
Parma Violet

Letting Go
Skullcap

Let Us Forget
Sweetbrier (Yellow)

Let's Take A Chance
Tulip (White)

Legal Matters
Buckthorn, Cascara, Celandine, Hickory Tree, Marigold,
Skunk Cabbage

Lenient
Lime Tree

Levity
Larkspur

Liberty
Bird of Paradise, Live Oak

Lies
Lily (Yellow)

Life
Lucerne, Lungwort, Pinecone

Life Direction
Camphor, Snowdrop

Lightening Protection
Holly

Lightness
Larkspur

Literary Debut
Tulip

Little Apple of Death
Manchineel Tree

Live for Me
Arborvitae

Live Life In The Fast Lane
Kudzu

Lively and Pure Affection
Carnation (Pink)

Living For Love
Carnation (White)

Logical Functioning
Chamomile

Loneliness
Anemone, Fungus, Heather

Long Beautiful
Begonia

Long Life
Chrysanthemum, Euonymus, Meadow Sage, Orchid, Sage

Longevity
Bamboo, Cypress Tree, Fig, Floss Flower, Lavender, Lemon, Maple Tree, Peach, Sage, Tansy

Longing
Camellia (Pink)

Look Up and Kiss Me
London Pride

Loss Of What Could Have Been
Daylily

Lost Love
Anemone, Tulip (White)

Love
Adam and Eve Root, Apple, Apricot, Aster, Avens, Avocado, Bachelor's Button, Balm of Gilead, Barley, Basil, Bean, Bedstraw, Beet, Black Cohosh, Bleeding Heart, Bloodroot, Brazil Nut, Canterbury Bells, Cardamom, Catnip, Chamomile, Catnip, Cherry, Chestnut Tree, Chickweed, Chili Pepper, China Berry, Cinnamon, Clove, Clover, Coltsfoot, Columbine, Copal, Coriander, Crape Myrtle, Crocus, Cymbidium Orchid, Daffodil, Devil's Bit, Dodder, Dragon's Blood, Dutchman's Britches, Elecampane, Elm Tree, Endive, Eryngo, Fairy Lily, Ferns, Fig, Fuzzy Weed, Gardenia, Gentian, Geranium, Ginger, Ginseng, Grass of Paradise, Heather, Hemp, Hibiscus, High John the Conqueror, Honeysuckle, Houseleek, Hyacinth, Indian Paintbrush, Japonica, Jasmine, Joe Pye Weed Jonquil, Juniper, Jupiter's Beard, Keys of Heaven, Lady's Mantle, Lavender, Leek, Lemon, Lemon Balm, Lemon Verbena, Lettuce, Licorice, Lilac, Liverwort, Lovage, Love In A Mist, Love Seed, Lucky Seed, Maidenhair Fern, Malva, Mandrake, Maple Tree, Marjoram, Meadowsweet, Michaelmas Daisy, Mimosa Tree, Mint, Mistletoe, Moonwort, Moss Rose, Mullein, Myrtle, Nuts, Orange Blossom, Orchid, Orris Root, Pansy, Papaya, Parsley, Pea, Peach, Pear, Peppermint, Periwinkle, Pimento, Plumeria, Poppy, Prickly Ash, Primrose, Purslane, Quince, Rain Lily, Raspberry, Rose (Red), Rose, Rose Mallow, Rosemary, Rose of Sharon, Rue, Rye, Sarsaparilla, September Flower, Saffron, Skullcap, Snake Root, Spearmint, Spiderwort, Starwort, St. John's Wort, Strawberry, Sugar Cane, Tamarind, Thyme, Tulip (red), Valerian, Vanilla, Venus Flytrap, Vervain, Vetivert, Violet, Wild Violet, Willow, Wormwood, Yarrow

Love at First Sight
Astilbe, Coreopsis, Gladiolus, Gloxinia, Rose, Rose (Lavender), Thornless Rose, Sword Lily

Love Attraction
Bleeding Heart, Dutchman's Britches, Hearts (White),
Monk's Head, Soldier's cap, Squirrel Corn

Love from a Son or Daughter
Clematis

Love From a Woman to a Man
African Daisy

Love in All Seasons
Gorse

Love in Idleness
Heartsease

Love Is Dangerous
Carolina Rose

Love Is Reciprocated
Ambrosia

Love Letters
Lily of the Nile

Love Luck
Aster

Love of Nature
Magnolia

Love of Variety
China Aster

Love Returned
Ambrosia, Bitterweed, Bloodweed, Ragweed

Love Undimished by Adversity
Dogwood

Loveliness
Dogwood, Gardenia, Smilax

Lovely
Carnation (White)

Lover
Cuckoo Flower

Lover's Charm
Almond

Love's Oracle
Dandelion

Lovers
Heather

Lovers' Tryst
Beech Tree

Loyal Love
Chrysanthemum, Daisy

Loyalty
Bamboo, Bluebell, Daisy, Ivy, Sunflower

Luck
Allspice, Aloe, Anise, Apple Blossom, Bamboo, Banyan, Bells of Ireland, Cabbage, Calamus, Camellia, Capers, Cinchona, Clover (White), Corn, Cotton, Daffodil, Daisy, Devil's Shoestring, Dill, Fern, Grains of Paradise, Hazel, Heather, Holly, Houseleek, Huckleberry, Irish Moss, Job's Tears, Kava-Kava, Lavender, Lucky Hand, Moss, Nuts, Orange, Orange Blossom, Persimmon, Pineapple, Pomegranate, Poppy, Purslane, Snakeroot, Strawberry, Vetivert, Violet

Luck in Fishing
Hawthorn

Lust
Avocado, Black Snakeroot, Cardamom, Carrot, Cyclamen, Dill, Hibiscus, Persian Violet, Capers, Caraway, Cattail, Celery, Daisy, Deerstongue, Devil's Bit, Endive, Garlic, Gorse, Blue Ginger, Ginseng, Grains of Paradise, Lemongrass, Licorice, Maguey, Mastic, Mint, Nettle, Olive, Onion, Patchouli, Pear, Periwinkle, Radish, Rose (Purple), Saffron, Sesame, Sugar Cane, Vanilla, Violet

Lust Protection
Cinnamon

Luster
Crowsfoot

Luxury
Horse Chestnut, Cymbidium Orchid

Magic
Angelica, Bird's Nest Fern, Ferns

Magnanimous
Delphinium, Orchid

Magnificence
Cymbidium Orchid, Orchid

Majesty
Crown Imperial, Elm Tree

Magnificent Beauty
Calla Lily

Make Haste
Dianthus

Male Luck / Maleness
Camellia

Malevolence
Asthma Weed, Indian Tobacco, Lobelia

Malicious Representation
Hellebore, Lenten Rose

Manifestations
Balm of Gilead, Dittany of Crete, Mastic

Manners
Rue

Many Children
Orchid

Many Interests
Begonia

Marital Affection
Lime

Marriage
Orange Blossom, , Linden Tree, Peony, Safflower,
Stephanotis, Verbena

Marriage/ Happy Marriage
Rosemary

Maternal Affection / Maternal Love
Carnation (Pink), Cinquefoil, Moss, Nasturtium

Matronly Grace
Cattleya Orchid

Mature Charm
Cattleya Orchid

Maturity
Oak Tree

Meanness
Cuscuta, Dodder of Thyme

Meditation
Abutilon, Bodhi, Chamomile, Daffodil, Gotu Kola, Hemp

Meekness
Birch Tree, Broom

Melancholy
Autumn Leaves, Cranesbill (Dark), Geranium, Geranium (Dark), Willow, Wild Daisy

Memories
Colchicum, Everlasting, Forget-Me-Not, Meadow Saffron, Periwinkle (Vinca), Sweet William

Memories of Childhood
Buttercup

Memory
Forget Me Not, Rosemary, Tulip

Mental Ability
Lily of the Valley

Mental Beauty
Clematis, Kennedia

Mental Prowess/ Mental Powers
Burnet, Caraway, Celery, Eyebright, Grape, Horehound, Mace, Mustard, Periwinkle, Rosemary, Rue, Summer Savory, Spearmint, Vanilla, Walnut Tree

Merry Heart
Apostle Plant

Message
Apostle Plant, Iris (Flags) Fleur de Lis, Winged Seeds (Any)

Mildness
Hibiscus, Mallow, Malva, Rose Mallow, Rose of Sharon, Althea

Mirth
Broom, Chrysanthemum, Crocus, Hops, Poinsettia, Saffron, Wild Grape

Misanthropy
Aconite, Wolfsbane

Misery
Calendula, Pot Marigold

Misplaced Devotion
Aloe

Misrepresentation
Dahlia

Mistrust
Lavender

Missive
Apostle Plant, Iris (Flags)

Mixed Feeling
Dog Rose

Mobility
Kudzu, Pine Tree, Walking Fern

Moderating Anger
Alyssum

Moderation
Azalea

Modest Genius
Creeping Cereus

Modest Love
Violet (Blue)

Modesty
African Violet, Alyssum, Aurinia, Calla Lily, Cosmos,
Cyclamen, Heartsease, Jasmine, Johnny Jump Up, Lilac, Lily
(White), Mimosa, Sweet Alison, Sweet Alyssum, Viola, Woad

Momentary Happiness
Spiderwort

Money
Chamomile, Flax, Honeysuckle, Flowering Kale, Maple Tree,
Millet, Orange Blossom, Periwinkle, Peruvian Lily, Poppy,
Alfalfa, Allspice, Almond, Bergamot, Blackberry, Bromeliad,
Bryony, Buckwheat, Calamus, Cascara, Cashew, Cedar Tree,
Cinquefoil, Clove, Clover, Comfrey, Dill, Dock, Fenugreek,
Fumitory, Ginger, Blue Ginger, Golden Seal, Goldenrod,
Gorse, Grains of Paradise, Grape, High John the Conqueror,
Honesty, Horse Chestnut, Iris (Blue), Irish Moss, Jasmine,
Lucky Hand, Marjoram, Mandrake, May Apple, Mint,
Moonwort, Moss, Oats, Onion, Orange, Oregon Grape,
Patchouli, Pea, Pecan Tree, Pine Tree, Pineapple, Poplar
Tree, Rattlesnake Root, Rice, Sarsaparilla, Sassafras, Sesame,
Snakeroot, Black Snakeroot, Vervain, Vetivert, Wheat,
Woodruff

Moonlight
Artemisia, Moonflower

Most Lovable
Ajuga, Bugle

Mother / Motherhood
Pussy Willow, Day Lily, Lily

Motherly Love
Balsam, Busy Lizzie, Impatiens, Jewel Weed, Our Lady's
Earrings, Patient Lucy, Policeman's Helmet, Sultana, Touch-
Me-Not

Motivation
Love In A Mist

Mourning
Cypress Tree, Rose (Dark Crimson)

Music
Alder Tree, Oats, Reeds

My Bane and My Antidote
Poppy (White)

My Best Days Are Past
Autumn Crocus, Colchicum, Meadow Saffron

My Compliments
Apostle Plant, Flags, Iris

My Destiny Is In Your Hands
Camellia

My Fortune Is Yours
Cinnamon

My Gratitude Exceeds Your Care
Dahlia

My Happiest Days Have Pasted
Meadow Saffron

My Heart Aches for You
Carnation, Carnation (Red), Dianthus

My Heart Is Yours
Peach Blossom

My Regrets Follow You to The Grave
Asphodel

Mysterious
Camas, Hyacinth (Wild), Quamash

Mystery
Rose (Blue)

Natural Beauty
Citron

Natural Grace
Gladiolus, Sword Lily

Nature
Magnolia

Neatness
Broom

Needing Protection
Gerbera Daisy

Neglected Beauty
Throatwort, Trachelium

Never Ceasing Remembrance
Everlasting, Statice

Never Despairing
Petunia

Never Judge Solely On Appearances
Coriander

Never Return
Rue

New Beginnings
Sage

New Ideas
Saxifrage

Newborn Baby
English Daisy

New Love
Rosebud

Night
Convolvulus Minor, Bindweed, Moon Vine, Moonflower

Nirvana
Bo Tree

No
Carnation (Any Bi-color), Carnation (Yellow), Snapdragon

No Change Until Death
Bay Leaf

Nobility
Cherry, Cloves, Edelweiss, Lily, Magnolia Tree

Not Funny
Oxalis, Sorrel, Wood Sorrel

Not So Bad As I Seem
Basket Lily, Ismene, Peruvian Daffodil, Sea Daffodil, Spider Lily

Novelty
Dahlia

Nuisance
Ragweed

Numerous Progeny
Orchid

Obedience
Balloon Flower, Chinese Bellflower

Objectivity
Groundsel

Obligation
Canterbury Bells

Oblivion
Poppy

Obsession
Rose (Black)

Obstacles
Hawthorn Tree, Mistletoe

Old Beau
Ice Plant

Omen / Sign
Cape Marigold

One Love
Arbutus, Madrone, Strawberry Tree

Only Deserve My Love
Champion Rose

Open Heart
Larkspur

Optimism/Optimistic
Chrysanthemum, Eustoma, Lisanthus, Prairie Gentian, Prairie Rose, Texas Bluebell, Tulip Gentian

Organization
Broom

Ornament
Hornbeam

Ostentation
Peony

Our Hearts Are United / Our Souls Are United
Phlox

Outgoing
Bluebell

Overcoming Difficulties
Mistletoe

Overcoming Fear
Aspen Tree

Pain
Blackthorn, Harebell

Painful Remembrance
Adonis, Pheasant's Eye

Painting
Auricula

Panache
Calla Lily

Parental Affection
Sorrel

Partiality
Apple Blossom

Participation
Double Dahlia

Passion
Apostle Plant, Arum, Azalea, Canterbury Bells (Red), Carnation (Laced), Carnation (Red), Dittany of Crete, Gorse, Iris, Lily, Poppy (Red), Rose, Rose (Purple), Rose (Red with one Yellow), Tulip

Passionate Interest
Orange Rose

Past
Meadow Saffron

Pastoral Poetry
Amaryllis

Paternal Error
Cardamom, Cuckoo Flower

Patience
Allium, Aster, Bed Straw Chamomile, Dock, Ox-Eye Daisy,
Shasta Daisy, Willow, Yew

Patriotism
Nasturtium, American Elm Tree

Peace
Bilberry, Blooming Sally, Buck Bean, Cattail, Cumin, Currant,
Gooseneck, Lavender, Loosestrife, Mistletoe, Olive,
Oregano, Hazel, Eryngo, Gardenia, Meadowsweet,
Pennyroyal, Saxifrage, Skullcap, Vervain, Violet

Peace and Prosperity
Fig, Gardenia

Peace and Victory
Olive Tree

Peacefulness
Cosmos

Peerless and Proud
Corn Cockle

Pensive Beauty
Golden Chain Tree, Laburnum

Pensiveness
Cowslip, Primrose

Perception of Reality
Gentian

Perfect Goodness
Strawberry

Perfect Happiness
Rose (Pink)

Perfect Lover
Camellia, Tulip

Perfected Loveliness
Camellia Japonica (White)

Perfection
Alyssum, Aurinia, White Camellia, Carnation, Dianthus,
Japonica, Pineapple, Pinks, Sweet William

Perfidy
Almond, Laurel

Perplexity
Love-In-A-Mist

Persecution
Mission Bells

Perseverance
Hydrangea, Magnolia Tree, Canary Grass, Yew

Persistence
Cushion Spurge, Euphorbia

Personal Achievement
Laurel

Personal Relationships
Forget Me Not

Persuasion
Althea, Marshmallow, Rose of Sharon

Pertinacity (Persistance)
Coltbur

Philosophy
Pine

Physician Plant
Chamomile

Piety
Amaranth

Pilgrimage
Plantain

Pity
Camellia, Pine Tree,

Platonic Love
Bittersweet, Black Locust

Playful
Bluebell, Eustoma, Gentian, Lisanthus, Prairie Rose

Playfulness
Buttercup, Delphinium, Hyacinth (Red or Pink)

Pleasantness
Alstromeria, Peruvian Lily

Pleasant Thoughts
Heartsease, Johnny Jump Up, Pansy

Please Believe Me
Rose (Pink)

Please Forgive Me
Hyacinth (Purple)

Pleasure
Poppy (Red), Tuberose

Pleasure and Pain
Dog Rose

Pleasure of Hope
Crocus

Pleasure without Alloy
Turtlehead

Pleasures of Memory
Periwinkle (White), Vinca

Poetry
Alder Tree, Amaryllis, Eglantine, Japanese Maple (Haiku), Sweet Briar, Wild Rose

Poise
Oriental Hellebore

Pomp
Dahlia

Popular Favor/Popularity
Begonia, Cistus, Kalanchoe

Popular Oracle
English Daisy

Positive Outlook
Wild Violet

Positive Perspectives
Sage

Positive Self-Image
Snowflake

Positive Thoughts
Pennyroyal

Potency
Banana, Palm Tree, Bean, Capers, Black Cohosh, Dates, Dragon's Blood, Olive, Palm Tree

Poverty - Clematis

Power
Artemisia, Cress, Crown Imperial, Cinnamon, Club Moss, Devil's Shoestring, Ebony, Gentian, Ginger, Roots, St. John's Wort

Pray for Me
Verbena

Prayer
Blueberry, Hyacinth (White), Reed

Precaution
Goldenrod

Preference
Apple, Apple Blossom, Rose-Scented Geranium

Presage
Cape Marigold

Present Preference
Apple-Scented Geranium

Presumption/Presumptuous
Snapdragon, Toadflax

Pretend to Love
Catchfly

Pretension
Amaranth, Coxcomb, Glasswort, Loosestrife

Pride
Amaryllis, Apple of Peru, Auricula, Carnation, Carnation (Pink), Dianthus, Ginger, Lilac, Lily, Shoo Fly Plant, Sunflower

Pride and Beauty
Carnations (Mixed Colors)

Pride of Birth
Crown Imperial

Privation
Myrobalan

Profit
Cabbage

Profits in Business
Pea

Progress
Oak Tree

Prohibition
Privet

Prolific
Fig Tree

Promise
Almond, Apple Blossom, Iris, Plum

Promise of Good Things to Come
Buds, Iris

Promptness
Gillyflower, Queen Anne's Thimbles, Stock

Prophecies
Linden Tree

Prophetic Dreams
Bracken, Buchu, Cinquefoil, Heliotrope, Jasmine, Marigold, Mimosa, Mugwort, Onion

Proposal of Love
Phlox

Prosperity
Alfalfa, Alkanet, Almond, Ash Tree, Banana, Beech Tree Bryony, Cattail, Lily, Nuts, Peony, Organ Grape

Prosperity and Plenty
Grape, Love-In-AMist, Wheat

Protection
Aaron's Beard, Acacia, African Violet, Agrimony, Ague Root, Aloe, Althea, Alum Root, Alyssum, Amaranth, Angelica, Arbutus, Asafetida, Ash Tree, Aurinia, Balm of Gilead, Bamboo, Barley, Basil, Bay, Bean, Bearded Crepis, Benzoin, Birch Tree, Bittersweet, Black Cohosh, Blackberry, Bloodroot, Blooming, Sally, Blue Ginger, Blueberry, Bodhi, Boneset, Boswellia, Broom, Bryony, Buckthorn, Buckwheat, Burdock, Cactus, Calamus, Caraway, Carnation, Carob, Cascara, Castor Bean, Cedar, Celandine, Chives, Chrysanthemum, Cinchona, Cinquefoil, Clove, Clover, Club Moss, Coconut, Coral Bells, Corn, Cotton, Cuckoo, Cumin, Curry, Cyclamen, Cypress Tree, Datura, Deerstongue, Devil's Bit, Devil's Shoestring, Dill, Dogwood, Dragon's Blood, Ebony, Elder, Elecampane, Eucalyptus, Euphorbia, Fennel, Fern, Feverfew, Figwort, Fir Tree, Flax, Fleabane, Foxglove, Frankincense, Garlic, Geranium, Ginseng, Gooseneck, Gorse, Gourd, Grain, Crass, Hazel, Heather (White), Hellebore (Black), Holly, Holly Berries, Honeysuckle, Horehound, Houseleek, Huckleberry, Hyacinth, Hypericum, Hyssop, Irish Moss, Ivy, Juniper, Juniper Tree, Jupiter's

Beard, Kava-Kava, Keys of Heaven, Lady's Slipper, Larch, Larkspur, Lavender, Leek, Lettuce, Liverwort, Loosestrife, Lotus, Lucky Hand, Mallow, Mandrake, Marigold, Marjoram, Masterwort, Mimosa, Mint, Mistletoe, Molukka Bean, Mugwort, Mullen, Mustard, Myrrh, Nettle, Norway Spruce Tree, Oak Tree, Olive, Onion, Orris Root, Papaya, Papyrus, Parsley, Pennyroyal, Peony, Pepper, Pepper Tree, Periwinkle, Persian Violet, Pimpernel, Pine Tree, Plantain, Primrose, Purslane, Quince, Radish, Raspberry, Rattlesnake Root, Rhubarb, Rice, Roots, Rosemary, Rowan Tree, Sage, Sandalwood, Snapdragon, Solomon's Seal, Spanish Moss, St. John's Wort, Sweet Alyssum, Sweet Gum Tree, Tamarisk, Thistle, Toadflax, Turnip, Valerian, Venus Flytrap, Vervain, Wax Plant, Willow, Wintergreen, Witch Hazel, Wolf's Bane, Woodruff, Wormwood, Yucca

Protection for Ships

Hawthorn

Protection for Travelers
Wormwood

Protection from Danger
Heather

Protection from Snakes
Juniper

Providence
Trefoil

Prudence
Ash, Mountain Ash

Psychic Powers
Acacia, Althea, Anise, Bay, Bistort, Borage, Celery,
Cinnamon, Citron, Elder Tree, Elecampane, Eyebright, Flax,
Ginger (Blue), Grass, Honeysuckle, Lemongrass, Mace,
Marigold, Mastic, Mugwort, Peppermint, Rose, Rowan Tree,
Saffron, Thyme, Wormwood, Yarrow

Psychic Workings
Uva Urse

Pure/Purity
Althea, Marshmallow, Abyssinian, Baby's Breathe, Broom,
White Carnation, Chaste Tree, Daisy, Edelweiss, Florist's
Nightmare, Gardenia, Jupiter's Beard, Keys of Heaven, Lilac,
Lily (White), Lily of the Valley, White Rose, Rosebud, Star of
Bethlehem, Sword Lily, Valerian, Water Lily

Pure Affection
Pinks

Pure and Ardent Love
Carnation (White)

Pure and Deep Love
Carnation, Dianthus

Pure and Lovely
Red Rosebud

Pure Heart
Baby's Breath

Pure Love
Carnation (Red), Cosmos

Purification
Alkanet, Asafetida, Avens, Bay, Benzoin, Birch Tree,
Bloodroot, Broom, Cedar Tree, Chamomile, Coconut, Copal,
Euphorbia, Fennel, Horseradish, Hyssop, Iris, Lavender,
Lemon, Lemon Verbena, Mimosa Tree, Parsley, Peppermint,
Rosemary, Sagebrush, Shallot, Thyme, Tobacco, Turmeric,
Valerian, Vervain, Yucca

Purifies Negativity and Evil
Gum Arabic

Purity
Gardenia
Purity of Heart
Water Lily

Quandary
Convolvulus

Quarrel
Broken Corn, Broken Straw

Questioning
Love-In-A-Mist

Quick-Sighted
Hawkweed

Radiant
Ranunculus

Rain
Bugle Lily, Cotton, Fern, Rice

Rain Magic
Pansy

Rain Making
Fern, Heather, Toadstool

Rare Beauty
Orchid

Rarity
Mandrake

Rashness
Butterfly Bush, Hyacinth

Readiness
Valerian (Red)

Ready-Armed
Gladiolus, Sword Lily

Reason
Goat's Rue

Rebirth
Rose (Black)

Rebuff
Dahlia (Yellow)

Recall
Geranium (Silver)

Recantation
Lotus Leaf

Reckless
Mandevilla

Reciprocated Love
Jerusalem Oak

Reconciliation
Bean, Filbert Nut, Florist's Nightmare, Hazel, Star of
Bethlehem,

Recovery from Illness
Pussy Willow

Reduces Fears
St. John's Wort, Wormwood

Refinement
Cornflower, Gardenia, Orchid, Sweet Sultan

Refusal
Anemone, Carnation (Striped), Lavender, Tansy

Regard
Buttercup, Cypress Tree, Daffodil, Jonquil

Regret
Asphodel, Bluebell, Colchicum, Elder Tree, Meadow Saffron,
Verbena (Purple)

Rejected/Rejection
Ice Plant, Carnation (Striped), Carnation (Yellow), Withered
Flowers

Rejected Suitor
Ice Plant

Rejoices and Comforts the Heart
Cicely

Rejuvenation
Lemon Balm

Relationships
Honesty

Relaxation
Apple, Currant, Gooseberry, Stitchwort

Release of Negativity
Forget-Me-Not

Relief
Balm of Gilead, Lemon Balm

Relieve My Anxiety
Hellebore, Christmas Rose, Lenten Rose

Religion
Lychnis, Maltese Cross, Passion Flower

Religious Enthusiasm
Lychnis

Religious Superstition
Aloe

Remember Me/Remembrance
Carnation (Pink or White), Chrysanthemum (White), Everlasting, Forget-Me-Not, Hydrangea, Marigold, Rosemary, Statice, Sweet Pea, Zinnia (Yellow)

Remorse
Bramble, Raspberry

Removing Obstacles
Chicory

Rendezvous
Chickweed, Pimpernel

Renewal
Yew

Resentment
Petunia

Reserve
Maple Tree, Sycamore Tree

Resignation
Cyclamen, Nasturtium, Persian Violet

Resilience
Bird's-foot Trefoil

Resistance
Tansy, Tremella Nestoc

Resoluteness
Sumac

Resolved to Win
Columbine (Purple)

Respect
Buttercup, Joe Pye Weed, Jonquil, Pea, Sage

Responsibility
Lemon Verbena

Rest
Hops

Restful
Chrysanthemum

Restless
Marigold

Restoration
Knotweed

Retaliation
Scotch Thistle

Retirement
Tulip Poplar

Retirement Happiness
African Blue Lily, Lily of the Nile

Return of a Friend is Desired
Balloon Flower, Bellflower, Delphinium

Return of Happiness
Lily of the Valley

Return Quickly
Corchorus

Reunion
Hazel

Reverie
Osmunda

Revenge
Trefoil, Clover, Birdsfoot Trefoil

Reverie
Flowering Fern

Reward of Merit
Bay Wreath, Laurel

Reward of Virtue
Crown or Garland of Roses

Rich in Charms
Buttercup

Riches
Buttercup, , Camellia, Chrysanthemum, Corn Blossom, Fern, Tea, Tiger Lily, Marigold, Wax Flower, Wheat

Righteousness
Genetian

Rigor
Lantana

Risque
Frilled Pansies

Role Reversal
Perilla

Romance
Azalea

Romantic Love
Grape Hyacinth

Royalty
Angrec, Tulip (Purple)

Rudeness
Coltbur

Rue
Carnation (Yellow)

Rune Magic
Bracken

Rupture
Blue Valerian

Rural Happiness
Tulip Poplar, Violet (Yellow)

Rustic Beauty
French Honeysuckle

Sacred Affection
Marigold

Sad Memories
Adonis

Sadness / Sorrow
Citron, Dead Leaves, Gerbera Daisy, Hyacinth (Purple), Yew Tree

Safe
Ginger

Safety
Broom, Traveler's Joy

Safety during Travel
Comfrey

Sanctuary
Rowan Tree

Satire
Prickly Pear

Scandal
Hellebore, Madder

Scholarship
Coral Bells, Cymbidium Orchid

Scorn
Carnations, Dianthus, Pinks, Sweet William

Sculpture
Hoya, Wax Plant

Sea Rituals
Ash Tree

Secrecy
Full Rose over Two Buds, Rose (White), Maidenhair Fern

Secret Admirer
Chrysanthemum (Yellow)

Secret Bond of Love
Maidenhair Fern

Secret Followers of Oscar Wilde
Green Canterbury Bells

Secret Love
Acacia, Gardenia, Maidenhair Fern, Mimosa Tree,
Motherwort

Secret Sweetness
Oxalis, Sorrel, Wood Sorrel

Seeking
Asparagus Fern

Self-Assurance
Oriental Hellebore

Self-Communication
Gentian

Self-Confidence
Aspen

Self-Determination
Wormwood

Self-Empowerment
Mullein

Self-Esteem
Basil, Coxcomb, Gentian

Self-Expression
Rue

Self-Image
Rue

Self-Knowledge
Honesty, Mullein

Self-Love
Daffodil, Narcissus

Self-Seeking
Clianthus

Self-Understanding
Wild Violet

Selfishness
Narcissus

Sense of Self
Mock Orange

Sensibility
Mimosa

Sensitivity / Sensitive
Lavender, Mimosa, Rue, Verbena (Scarlet)

Sensuality
Jasmine

Sentimental Recollections
Artemisia

Separation
Blackthorn, Carolina Jasmine, Datura, Trumpet Flower

Serenade
Dew Plant

Serenity
Buck Bean, Chamomile, Currant, Willow

Sexual Liberation
Carnation (Pink)

Sexual Passion
Hibiscus, Mallow, Malva, Rose Mallow, Rose of Sharon

Shame
Hawthorn Tree, Peony

Shared Secrets
African Daisy

Sharpness
Laurel Tree

Sharpness of Temper
Barberry

Shelter
Bird's Nest Fern

Showy
Lisianthus

Shyness
Everlasting Pea, Four O'clock, Grass Pea, Peony, Peach
Rose, Sensitive Plant, Sweet Pea, Viola, Violet

Shyness Reduction
Oriental Hellebore

Sibling Relationships
Nettle

Sickness
Anemone

Silence
Belladonna, Nightshade, Rose (White)

Silliness
Celosia, Cockscomb, Cranesbill, Geranium

Simple Pleasure
Huckleberry

Simplicity
Single Rose, Wild Rose, Daisy, English Daisy, Anemone,
Cicely, Fern, Honesty

Sincerity
Bird's Nest Fern, Chervil, Fairy Lily, Fern, Gladiolus,
Honesty, Hyacinth, Japonica, Money Plant, Rain Lily, Satin
Flower, Sword Lily, Windflower, Zephyr Lily

Singularity
Celosia, Coxcomb

Slighted Love
Yellow Chrysanthemum

Skill
Coneflower, Spider Orchid

Sky
Coleus

Slander
Hellebore, Lenten Rose

Sleep
Chamomile, Cinquefoil, Datura, Hops, Lavender, Lettuce, Peppermint, Poppy, Purslane, Rosemary, Thyme, Valerian, Vervain

Slighted Love
Yellow Chrysanthemum

Snare
Arum, Catchfly, Dragon Plant

Softness
Lamb's Ears

Solitude
Bachelor's Button, Basket Flower Bluebottle, Boutonniere Flower, Cornflower, Fungus, Globeflower, Heath, Heather, Hurtsickle, Lavender, Lichen

Sooths the Heart
Lavender

Soothing
Dill, Milk Weed

Sophistication
Calla Lily

Sorcery
Nightshade

Sorrow
Aloe, Asphodel, Purple Hyacinth (Puurple), Iris (Yellow), Bluebell, Yew

Sorrowful Memories
Adonis, Blooddrops, Pheasant's Eye, Asclepius

Sorry I Can't Be with You
Striped Carnation

Souls United
Phlox

Sourness/Sourness of Temper
Barberry

Sparkle
Amaryllis

Speak Your Mind
Borage

Spectacular
Mexican Sage

Spell Breaking
Bamboo

Spirit Calling
Sweetgrass

Spirited
Freesia

Spiritual Beauty
Cherry Blossom

Spiritual Confidence
Snowdrop

Spiritual Energy
Pine Tree

Spirituality
African Violet, Cherry Blossom, Gourd, Cinnamon,
Frankincense (Boswellia), Gardenia, Myrrh, Passionflower,
Sandalwood

Splendid Beauty
Amaryllis

Splendor
Blood Flower, Blood Lily, Cape Tulip, Cape Lily (Red),
Cardinal Flower, Catherine Wheel, Fireball Lily, Poison Root,
Turk's Cap

Spontaneous
Begonia

Sporting
Foxtail, Kill Weed, Long Purples, Rainbow Weed, Red Sally,
Rosy Strife, Sage Willow, Salicaire, Spiked Soldiers, Willow
Weed

Sports
Hyacinth

Stability
Cress

Stateliness
Foxglove

Stay As Sweet As You Are
Narcissus

Stay Out of my Way
Kudzu

Steadfast/Steadfastness
Bamboo, Globe Amaranth, Wisteria, Zinnia (Scarlet)

Steadfast Piety
Wild Geranium

Strength
Bamboo, Bay, Cedar Tree, Coneflower, Carnation,
Everlasting Pea, Fennel, Garlic, Master Wort, Mugwort,
Mulberry, Oak Leaf, Oak Tree, Pennyroyal, Plantain, Saffron,
Snapdragon, St. John's Wort, Sweet Pea, Tea, Thistle,
Toadflax

Strength of Character
Gladiolus, Sword Lily

Stress Relief
Hellebores

Strength of Mind
Walnut

Strength to Grow Thin
Fennel

Stoicism
Box

Stratagem
Walnut Tree

Stress Release
Dandelion

Stress Relief
Nettle

Studious Pursuit
Olive

Stupidity
Cranesbill, Geranium, Geranium (Scarlet), Geranium

Submission
Grass, Harebell, Peach

Success
Apple of Peru, Bramble, Clover, Coronilla, Crown Vetch, Dogwood Tree, Ginger, High John the Conqueror, Laurel, Lavender, Leadwort, Lemon Balm, Marsh Rosemary, Palm Tree, Palm Leaves, Plumbago, Poinsettia, Poppy Yellow), Rosemary, Rowan Tree, Sea Lavender, Shoo Fly Plant, Solidago, Statice

Success Everywhere
Baby Blue Eyes

Success to You
Crown Vetch

Success Will Crown Your Wishes
Coronilla

Succor (Help)
Juniper Tree

Sun
Marigold, Sunflower

Sunny Disposition
Chamomile

Superior Merit
Moss Rose

Superstition
Aurilica, Hypericum, St. John's Wort,

Support
Black Bryony, Goldenrod, Lady's Seal, Lamb's Ears

Susceptibility
Wax Plant

Surprise
Betony, Lamb's Ears, Truffle

Suspicion
Lavender, Mushroom

Sweet and Secret Love
Honey Flower

Sweet Disposition
Honeysuckle, Hibiscus

Sweet Dreams
Closed Gentian, Phlox

Sweet Remembrance / Memories
Periwinkle, Vinca

Taste (Fashion/Style)
Fuchsia (Red)

Tears
Helenium

Technology
Red Clover

Temperance
Azalea

Temptation
Apple, Apple Blossom, Quince

Tenacity
Ivy

Tender and Quick Emotions
Verbena

Tender Memories
Sweet Pea

Tenderness
Sweet Pea

Tension Relief
Oriental Hellebore

Testing
Holly

Thank You/ Thanks
Fleabane, Parsley, Rose (Deep Pink)

Thank You for a Good Time
Sweet Pea

Thankfulness
Agrimony, Bellflower

The Sun Is Always Shining When I'm With You
Daffodil

Thee Only Do I Love
Arbutus

There's Sunshine in Your Smile
Tulip (Yellow)

Think of Me
Cedar, Clover, Heartsease, Johnny Jump Up, Pansy

Thinking of an Absent Friend
Barberton Daisy, Gerbera Daisy, Zinnia, Zinnia (Mixed)

Thinking of You
Bellflower , Pansy, Zinnia (Mixed)

Thinness
Fennel

Thought
Pansy

Thoughtfulness
Almond Tree, Orchid

Thoughtless
Mandevilla

Thoughts of Absent Friends
Zinnia

Thoughts of Heaven
Viburnum

Thy Smile I Aspire To
Rose

Time
Fir Tree, Pine Tree, White Poplar Tree

Timidity
Amaryllis, Four O'clock, Marvel of Peru

Token of Affection
Ox-eye Daisy, Viburnum

Tolerance
Daphne, Cuckoo Flower

Touch Me Not
Burdock, Touch-Me-Not

Tranquility
Artemisia, Madder, Mudwort, Mugwort, Sagebrush, Sedum, Stonecrop, Wormwood

Transformation
Ash Tree, Holly

Transience
Morning Glory

Transient Beauty
Night Blooming Cereus

Transient Impressions
Withered White Rose

Transitions
Yew

Transmutation
Yucca

Transport
Gardenia

Transport of Joy
Gardenia, Jasmine

Travel
Lucky Hand, Mint, Stephanotis

Traveler's Luck
Eryngo

Treachery
Bilberry, Mountain Laurel, Whortleberry

Treasure Finding
Cowslip

Tree of Life
Arbor Vitae

Tree of Mothers
Paper Birch

Trials
Holly

Trinity
Three-leaf Clover

Triteness
Quince

Triumph over Winter
Eastern Hemlock

Trouble
Marigold

True Friendship
Oak-leaf Geranium

True Love
Forget Me Not, Rose (Single Red)

True Love Forever
Forget-Me-Not

Trust/Trusting
Aster, Chrysanthemum (white), Daisy, Freesia, Tulip (red)

Trustfulness
Ivy

Trustworthiness
Honesty

Trust Me
Bronze Chrysanthemum

Truth
Anemone, Bittersweet, Bluebell, Bloom (White),
Chrysanthemum (White), Nightshade

Unanimity
Phlox

Unceasing Remembrance
Artemisia, Cudweed

Uncertainty
Bindweed, Morning Glory, Mock Orange, Narcissus

Unchangeable
Globe Amaranth

Unchanged for Eternity
Clematis

Unchanging Friendship
Arborvitae, Catchfly

Unchanging Love
Arborvitae, Balloon Flower, Chinese Bellflower

Unconscious Beauty
Burgundy Rose

Understanding
Hydrangea, Lemon Balm, Mace

Understanding Animal Languages
Cloth of Gold

Undying Love
Umbrella Pine Tree

Uneasiness
Marigold

Unexpected Meeting
Cranesbill, Lemon Geranium

Unfading Beauty
Carnation

Unfading Love
Anemone

Unfaithful
Evening Primrose, Oenothera

Unforgettable
Carnation (Pink)

Unfortunate Love
Pincushion Flower

Union
Straw

Unite Against Evil
Verbena (Scarlet)

Unity
Allium, Phlox, Rose, Rose (Red and White)

Secret Meanings of Flowers

Unobtrusive Loveliness
Grape Hyacinth, White Hyacinth

Unpretending Excellence
Camellia Japonica (Red)

Unpretentiousness
Pasque Flower

Unreliable
Carnation (Purple)

Unrequited Love
Begonia, Bleeding Heart, Buttercup, Cypress Tree, Daffodil, Jonquil

Untiring Energy
Salvia (Red)

Uprightness
Bamboo

Useful Knowledge
Parsley

Uselessness
Meadowsweet

Utility
Grass, Dried Flax

Valor
Apostle Plant, Iris (Flags),

Vanity
Cypress Tree

Variety
Aster, Calico Plant, Michaelmas Daisy, Multi-Colored
Flowers of Any Kind, Mundi Rose, September Flower,
Starwort

Varying Course of Life
Marigold with Red Flowers

Venerable
Dusty Miller

Verbal Communication
Snapdragon

Verity
Nightshade

Vice
Darnel

Victory
Mountain Laurel, Nasturtium, Palm Leaves, Palm Tree,
Spirea, Woodruff

Victory in Battle
Nasturtium

Vigilance
Wild Hyacinth, Pretty Face, Starflower

Virtue
African Violet, Damask Violet, Dame's Gillyflower, Dame's Rocket, Dame's Violet, Mint, Mother of the Evening, Night-Scented Gillyflower, Pineapple Sage, Summer Lilac, Sweet Rocket

Vitality
Apple, Broom, Gorse

Visions
Angelica, Coltsfoot, Crocus, Hemp, Kava-Kava

Vivacity
Houseleek

Voice of the Heart
Mandevilla

Voluptuousness
Tuberose, Moss Rose

Voluptuous Love
Moss Rose

Voraciousness
Bluebonnet, Lupine

Vows
Stock

Vulgar Minds
African Marigolds

Wantonness
Buddleia, Butterfly Bush

War
Achillea

Warding
Mistletoe

Warmth
Feverfew, Peppermint

Warmth of Heart / Warmhearted
Cyclamen (White), Rose

Warning
Aconite, Auld Wife's Huid, Begonia, Bellflower, Canterbury Bells, Friar's Cap, Ginger , Goldenrod, Hand Flower, Monkshood, Rhododendron, Yarrow

Warrior Spirit
Aspin, Columbine

Watchfulness
Azalea, Viola

Weak but Winning
Moschatel

Weakness
Musk Plant

Wealth
Basil, Bloom, Chrysanthemum, Heliotrope, Mum, Pomegranate, Poppy (Yellow), Ulster Marry

Wealth Is Not Always Happiness
Auricula

Wedded Love
Ivy

Wedding
Stephanotis

Wedding Will Follow Shortly
Honeysuckle

Welcome
Euphorbia, Mistletoe, Pineapple, Safflower, Spurge, Wisteria

Welcome Fair Stranger
Wisteria

Welcome Home Drunk Husband
Hen and Chicks, Sedum

Welcome to New Home
Juniper

Well- Being
Delphinium

Well -Spoken
Bluebell, Eustoma, Lisanthus, Prairie Gentian, Prairie Rose, Tulip Gentian

Well -Trodden Path
Plantain

Whimsical
Carnation (Purple)
Whimsy
Bells of Ireland, London Pride

Will You Accompany Me?
Stephanotis

Will Your Wish Be Granted?
Verbena

Wind
Broom, Saffron

Winter
Gueleder Rose

Wisdom
Aloe Almond, Apostle Plant, Bilberry, Bodhi, Hazel, Iris, Mulberry (White), Sage, Salvia (Blue), Sunflower

Wise Administration
Pear

Wish/ Wishes
Bamboo, Foxglove, White Heather, Beech Tree, Buckthorn, Dandelion, Dogwood, Ginseng, Grains of Paradise, Hazel, Job's Tears, Peach, Pomegranate, Sage, Sunflower, Violet, Walnut

Wishes Granted
Loosestrife

Wishes Will Come True
Coppertip, Crocosmia, Falling Star, Heather. Montbretia

Wistfulness
Blue Rose

Withered Hopes
Garden Anemone

Wit
Hellebore, Lenten Rose, Lychnis, Lemon Balm
With Love
Chrysanthemum

With Me You Are Safe
Ash Tree

Without Hope
Cypress Tree

Womanhood
Azalea

Woman's Love
Carnation, Carnation (Pink), Dianthus

Wonder
Pine or Fir Tree

Wonderful
Four O'clock, Marvel of Peru

Work
Red Clover

Worldliness
Clianthus

Worldly Goods
Wheat

Worried
Red Columbine

Worship
Heliotrope

Worth
White Camellia

Worth Beyond Beauty
Alyssum, Aurinia, Sweet Alison, Sweet Alyssum

Worth Sustained by Affection
Pink Convolvulus

Worthy of Praise
Fennel

Yes
Any solid color Carnation

Yielding
Lime Tree

You Are a Prophet
Hypericum

You Are a Wonderful Friend
Chrysanthemum

You Are Cold
Hydrangea

You Are Dazzling, But Dangerous
Snapdragon

You Are Delicious
Strawberry

You Are Everything to Me
Rose

You Are False
Foxglove

You Are Lovely
Gardenia

You Are Merry
Mundi Rose

You Are My Divinity
Cowslip, Primrose, Shooting Stars

You Are Perfect
Pineapple

You Are Splendid
Tall Sunflower

You Are Unfair
Gentian

You Are Unjust
Gentian

You Are Wonderful
Cowslip, Primrose

You Flatter Me
Orchid

You Have Disappointed Me
Carnation (Yellow)

You Have Listened To Scandal
Hellebore, Lenten Rose

You Have No Claims
Pasque Flower

You Light up My Life
Feverfew

You Love Yourself Too Much
Narcissus

You May Hope
Rose Leaf

You Occupy my Thoughts
Heartsease, Johnny Jump Up, Pansy

You Pierce My Heart
Gladiolus

You Please All
Currants

You Are the Only One I Love
Arbutus

You Will Cause My Death
Hemlock

You Will Succeed
Goldenrod

You Will Always Be Beautiful To Me
Stock

Your Blush Has Won Me
Azalea

Your Friendship Is Agreeable And Pleasing
Soy Bean

Your Friendship Is Valued
Apostle Plant, Iris

Your Frown Will Destroy Me
Currant

Your Hand for the Next Dance
Ivy Geranium

Your Image is Engraven on My Heart
Euonymus, Spindle Tree

Your Looks Freeze Me
Ice Plant, Dark Geranium

Your Love Is Returned
Ambrosia, Bitterweed, Bloodweed, Ragweed

Your Presence Sooths Me
Milk Vetch, Petunia

Your Qualities Surpass Your Charms
Mignonette

Your Simple Elegance Charms Me
Diosma

Your Thoughts Are Dark
Nightshade

Your Whims Are Unbearable
Bee Balm, Bergamot, Monarda

Your Wiles Are Irresistible
Bergamot

You Are the Only One
Daffodil

Youth
Buttercup, Catchfly, Cowslip, Foxglove, Lilac, Primrose,
Evening Primrose, Damask Rose, Rosebud, Rosemary,
Vervain

Youthful Beauty
Daisy

Youthful Gladness
Crocus

Youthful Innocence
White Lilac

Youthful Love
Red catchfly

You Have Made My Life Complete
Lilly of the Valley

Zeal
Elderberry

Zealousness
Elder Tree

Zest – Lemon

Brenda Jenkins Kleager

PLANT NAMES

Aaron's Beard
Invincibility, Protection

Abatina
Fickleness

Abor Vitae
Unchanging Love, Everlasting Friendship

Abutilon
Meditation

Abyssinian
Courage, Purity, Sweetness

Acacia
Beauty, Beauty in Retirement, Chaste Love, Concealed Love, Friendship, Hidden Love, Innocence, Secret Love

Acacia, Pink
Grace

Acacia, Rose or White
Elegance, Friendship

Acanthus
Artifice, Arts, Fine Arts

Achillea
Healing, Heartache Relief, War

Achillea Millifolia
War

Acacia
Protection, Psychic Powers

Acanthus
The arts

Aconite
Misanthropy, Warning

Adam and Eve Roots
Happiness, Love

Adder's Tongue
Healing, Jealousy

Adonis
Sad Memories, Painful Recollections

African Blue Lily
Retirement Happiness

African Daisy
Innocence, Love from Woman to Man, Shared Secrets

African Violet
Admiration, Delicate Love Connection, Faithfulness, Modesty, Protection, Spirituality, Virtue

Agaric
Fertility

Ageratum
Delay, Faithful Love

Agrimony
Gratitude, Protection, Sleep, Thankfulness

Ague Root
Protection

Alder Tree
Arts, Creativity, Guidance, Inspiration, Music, Poetry

Alfalfa
Anti-hunger, Money, Prosperity

Alkanet
Prosperity, Purification

Allium
Humility, Patience, Unity

Allspice
Benevolence, Compassion, Healing, Luck, Money

Almond
Heedlessness, Hope, Imprudence, Indiscretion, Lover's
Charm, Money, Perfidy, Promise, Prosperity, Wisdom

Almond Tree
Concealed Love, Hope, Thoughtlessness

Almond, Flowering
Hope

Aloe
Bitterness, Dejection, Good Luck, Grief, Healing, Integrity,
Luck, Misplaced Devotion, Protection, Sorrow, Wisdom

Alstroemeria / Peruvian Lily
Friendship, Pleasantries

Althea
Consumed by Love, Healing, Honesty, I am deeply in love,
Persuasion, Purity, Protection, Psychic Powers

Alum Root
Challenge, Protection

Alyssum
Anger Management, Excellence beyond beauty, Modesty,
Perfection, Protection, Worth Beyond Beauty

Amaranth / Globe Amaranth
Foppery, Healing, , Immortal love, Immortality, Invisibility,
Piety, Pretension, Protection, Unchangeable

Amaranthus
Heartless, Hopeless

Amaryllis
Drama, Haughtiness, Pastoral Poetry, Poetry, Pride, Sparkle,
Splendid Beauty, Timidity

Ambrosia
Love is Returned

Amethyst
Admiration

Anemone
Anticipation, Desertion, Estranged Love, Expectation,
Fading Love, Forsaken, Fragile, Health, Loneliness, Lost
Love, Truth, Sickness, Sincerity, Abandonment, Unfading
Love, Withered hopes

Anemone, Garden
Faith, Belief

Anemone, Japanese
Abandonment, Refusal

Angelica
Healing, Inspiration, Magic, Protection, Visions

Angel's Trumpet
Deceit

Angrec
Royalty

Anise
Luck, Psychic Powers

Anthurium/Flamingo Flower
The Heart

Apostle Plant
Eloquence, Faith, Friendship, Hope, Inspiration, Message,
Missive, My compliments, Passion, Promise, Valor, Wisdom,
Your Friendship is Valued

Apple
Concord, Garden Magic, Healing, Immortality, Love,
Temptation, Preference, Fame speaks well of him

Apple Blossom
Better things to Come, Fame, Future, Healing, Health, Hope,
Luck, Partiality, Preference, Promise, Relaxation, Temptation,
Vitality

Apple of Peru
Dignity, Pride, Success

Apricot
Distrust, Doubt, Love

Arbor Vitae
Everlasting Friendship, Tree of Life, Unchanging Friendship, Tree of Life

Arbutus
Faithfulness, One love, Protection, Thee only do I love, You are the only one I love

Armenia
Sympathy

Artemisia
Power, Dignity, Moonlight, Sentimental Recollection, Unceasing Remembrance

Arum
Ardor, Ferocity and Deceit, Passion, Snare

Asafetida
Protection, Purification

Asclepius
Remembrance, Sorrow

Ash Tree
Change, Destiny, Dignity, Fate, Grandeur, Growth, Health, Prosperity, Protection, Prudence, Sea Rituals, Transformation, With me you are safe

Ash-leafed Trumpet Flower
Separation

Asparagus
Fascination

Asparagus Fern
Curiosity, Seeking

Aspen Tree
Anti-Theft, Courage, Eloquence, Excess of Sensibility, Fear, Lamentation, Overcoming Fear, Self-confidence, Warrior Spirit

Asphodel
Forgiveness, My regrets follow you to the grave, Regret, Sorrow

Aster
Afterthought, Charming, Contentment, Daintiness, Diversity, Femininity, Grace, I'm not sure you've been faithful, Love, Luck in Love, Patience, Trusting, Variety

Aster, China
Love of Variety, Fidelity, I will think of you

Aster, Double
I share your sentiments

Aster, Single
I will think about it

Aster, White
Afterthought

Asthma Weed / Sticky-Weed
Arrogance, Malevolence

Astilbe
I'll still be waiting, Love at first sight

Auld Wife's Huid
Warning

Auricula
Avarice, Dejection, Painting, Pride, Sorrow, Superstition,
Wealth is not always happiness

Aurinia
Anger Management, Excellence beyond Beauty, Modesty,
Perfection

Autumn Leaves
Melancholy

Avens
Love, Purification

Avocado
Beauty, Love, Lust

Azalea
Abundance, Caution, Femininity, Forbearance, Fragile
Passion, Moderation, Passion, Romance, Take care of
yourself, Take care while I'm away, Temperance,
Watchfulness, Womanhood, Your blush has won me

Baby Blue Eyes
Success Everywhere

Baby's Breath
Cleverness, Constancy, Festivity, Happiness, Innocence,
Purity, Pure Heart, Gaiety

Bachelor's Button
Anticipation, Blessings of being single, Celibacy, Delicacy, Hope in love, Independence, Love, Solitude, Delicacy

Balloon Flower
Obedience, Unchanging love, Honesty, Return of a Friend is Desired

Balm
I long for your company, Joke, Sympathy
Balm of Gilead
Cure, Healing, Love, Manifestations, Protection, Relief

Balm, Lemon
Healing, Love, Success, Wit, Understanding, Fun, Relief, Rejuvenation, Sympathy

Balsam
Ardent Love, Come to Me, Impatience, Motherly Love

Balsam, Yellow
Impatient

Bamboo
Grace, Longevity, Loyalty, Luck, Protection, Steadfastness, Strength, Wishes, Uprightness

Banana
Fertility, Potency, Prosperity

Banyan Tree
Luck

Barberry
Sharpness of temper, Sourness

Barberton Daisy
Thoughts of Absent Friends

Barley
Healing, Love, Protection

Basil
Animosity, Best Wishes, Creativity, Flying, Give me your good wishes, Hatred, Healing, Love, Protection, Self-esteem, Wealth

Basket Flower
Anticipation, Blessings of being single, Celibacy, Independence, Solitude

Basket Lily
Elope with Me, I'm not as bad as I seem

Bay
Healing, Protection, Psychic powers, Purification, Strength

Bay Leaf
No change until death

Bay Tree
Glory

Bay Wreath
Reward of Merit

Bayberry / Wax Myrtle
Discipline, Instruction, Good luck

Bean
Love, potency, Protection, Reconciliation

Bedstraw
Love, Patience

Bee Balm / Monarda
Your whims are unbearable, Compassion, Sweet Virtues

Beech Tree
Affluence, Lovers' Tryst, Prosperity, Wishes

Beet
Love

Begonia
Beware, Dark Thoughts, Deep Thoughts, Fanciful Nature, Many Interests, Spontaneous, Take care while I'm away, Warning, Popular, Long beautiful, Unrequited love

Begonia, Strawberry
Cleverness

Bell Flower
Acknowledgment, Aspiring, Consistency, Gratitude, Grief, Humility, I wish to speak to you, Indiscretion, Return of a Friend is Desired, Thankfulness, Thinking of you, Warning

Belladonna
Astral projection, Drama, Silence

Bells of Ireland
Good Luck, Whimsy

Belvedere
I declare war against you

Benzoin
Protection, Purification

Bergamot
Money, Your whims are unbearable, Your wiles are irresistible

Betony
Surprise

Bilberry
Calmness, Clarity, Comunication, Peace, Treachery, Wisdom

Bindweed
Bonds, Eminence, Extinguished hope/s, Humility, Insinuation, Night, Uncertainty

Birch Tree (Paper Birch)
 Beginnings, Change, Elegance, Gracefulness, Meekness, Protection, Purification, Tree of Mothers

Birch (Weeping White Birch)
Beauty

Bird of Paradise
Faithfulness, Good Perspective, Liberty, Magnificence

Bird's Nest Fern
Confidence, Magic, Shelter, Sincerity

Birdsfoot Trefoil
Revenge

Bistort
Fertility, Psychic Powers

Bittersweet
Healing, Platonic Love, Protection, Truth

Bitterweed
Love Returned/ Your love is Returned

Black Bryony
Helpfulness, Support

Black Locust Tree
Platonic Love

Black Sampson
Healing

Blackberry
Dangerous Pride, Healing, Money, Protection

Black-Eyed Susan
Encouragement, Justice

Blackthorn
Adversity, Conflict, Difficulty, Pain, Separation

Bladder Nut Tree
Amusement, Frivolity

Blanket Flower
Joy

Blazing Star
Enthusiasm, I'll try again

Bleeding Heart
Elegance, Fidelity, Love, Love Attraction, Unrequited Love

Bloedblom
Glory, Splendor

Blood Flower
Glory, Let me go, Splendor

Blood Drops
Sorrowful Memories

Bloodroot
Love, Protection, Purification

Blood Weed
Love Returned/ Your love is Returned

Bloom (Chrysanthemum)
Cheerfulness, Wealth, You are a wonderful friend

Bloom, Red
I love you

Bloom, White
Truth

Blooming Sally
Peace, Protection

Blue Woodruff
Humility

Bluebell
Constancy, Faithfulness, Fidelity, Gratitude, Humility,
Kindness, Loyalty, Luck, Regret, Sorrow, Truth

Blueberry
Protection, Prayer

Bluebonnet
Imagination, Voraciousness

Bluebottle
Anticipation, Blessings of being single, Celibacy,
Independence, Solitude

Bluet
Contentment

Bo Tree
Buddhism, Nirvana

Bodhi
Fertility, Meditation, Protection, Wisdom

Boneset
Protection

Borage
Abruptness, Bluntness, Courage, Directness, Psychic powers,
Talent

Boston Fern
Fascination

Bottlebrush
Delicacy

Boutonniere Flower (Centaurea)
Anticipation, Blessings of being single, Celibacy,
Independence, Solitude

Bouvardia
Enthusiasm

Box
Constancy

Box Tree / Boxwood
Constancy in Friendship, I believe in your constancy,
Stoicism

Bracken
Healing, Prophetic Dreams, Rune magic

Bramble
Celebration, Envy, Holiness, Remorse, Success

Brazil Nut
Love

Bridal Wreath
Come to Me, Desire to Travel, Happiness in Marriage

Briar
Envy

Bromeliad
Money, Protection

Broom
Divination, Healing, Humility, Meekness, Mirth, Neatness,
Organization, Protection, Purification, Purity, Safety, Vitality,
Wind Spells

Browallia
Admiration, Could you bear poverty?

Brown-Eyed Susan
Impartiality

Bryony
Image Magic, Money, Prosperity, Protection

Bryony, Black
Be my support

Bubby Bush
Benevolence, Generosity

Buchu
Prophetic Dreams, Psychic Powers

Buck Bean
Calmness, Calm Repose, Peace, Serenity

Buckthorn
Legal Matters, Protection, Wishes

Buckwheat
Money, Protection

Buds
Promise of good things to come

Bugle Lily / Ajuga
Anticipation, Cheers the Heart, Most Lovable, Rain

Bugloss
Falsehood

Bulrush
Docility, Indiscretion

Bumblebee Orchid
Industry

Burdock
Importunity, Protection, Touch-Me-Not

Burgundy
Unconscious Beauty

Burnet
Merry heart, Joy

Busy Lizzie (Impatiens)
Impatience, Motherly Love

Buttercup
Cheerfulness, Childish ingratitude, Childishness, Chivalry,
Desire for riches, I am dazzled by your charms, Ingratitude,
Memories of childhood, Playfulness, Regard, Respect, Riches,
Rich in charms Unrequited love, Youth

Butterfly Bush / Buddleia
Healing, Rashness, Wantonness

Butterfly Weed
Heartache Relief, Let me go

Button Snake Root
Enthusiasm, I'll try again

Cabbage
Luck, Profit

Cactus
Affection, Bravery, Chastity, Desire, Endurance, Grandeur,
Protection, Warmth

Caladium
Delight, Great Joy

Calamus
Healing, Luck, Money, Protection

Calendula / Pot Marigold
Affection, Cares, Constancy, Disquietude, Grief, Health,
Jealousy, Joy, Misery, Remembrance, Sun

Calico Plant
Variety

Calla Lily
Beauty, Feminine Modesty, Magnificent Beauty, Modesty,
Royalty, Sophistication, Panache

Calycanthus
Benevolence, Generosity

Camas
Mysterious

Camellia
Beauty, Contentment, Excellence, Gift to a man,
Graciousness, Gratitude, Luck, Male luck, Maleness, My

destiny is in your hands, Perfected loveliness, Perfect lover, Perfection, Pity, Riches

Camellia, Pink
Longing

Camellia, Red
Alas my poor heart, Beauty, Flame, Innate warmth, Passion, Unpretending excellence

Camellia, White
Adoration, Beauty, Perfected Loveliness, Perfection, Worth

Campanula
Gratitude

Camphor
Chastity, Divination, Health

Canary Grass
Cleansing, Determination, Life Direction, Perseverance

Candytuft
Architecture, Balance, Indifference

Canna Lily
Great Beauty

Canterbury Bells
Acknowledgment, Consistency, Constancy, Fascination, Gratitude, Grief, Humility, Indiscretion, Love, Obligation, Thankfulness, Warning

Canterbury Bells, Red
Deep Romantic Love, Passion

Canterbury Bells, Green
Secret Followers of Oscar Wild

Crape Myrtle
Eloquence

Cape Tulip
Glory, Splendor

Capers
Luck, Potency

Caraway
Anti-Theft, Health, Infidelity Prevented, Lust, Mental
powers, Protection,

Cardamom
Love, Lust

Cardinal Flower
Distinction, Honor, Splendor

Cardinal Vine
Busybody

Carnation
Admiration, Ardent and Pure Love, Beauty, Goodness,
Bonds of Love, Chivalry, Devotion, Faithfulness, Fascination,
Finesse, Gallantry, Grant Me a Smile, Healing, My heart aches
for You, Perfection, Pride, Protection, Pure and Deep Love,
Scorn, Strength, Woman's Love, Unfading Beauty

Carnation, Any Bi-color
No!

Carnation, Any Solid Color
Yes!

Carnation, Deep Red
Alas for my poor heart

Carnation, Laced
Passion

Carnation, Mauve
Dreams of fantasy

Carnation, Mixed Colors
Beauty, Energy, Health, Pride

Carnation, Pink
Always on my Mind, Beauty, Encouragement, Friendship, Gratitude, I Will always Remember You, Maternal Love, Lively and Pure Affection, Pride, Remembrance, Sexual Liberation, Unforgettable, Woman's Love

Carnation, Purple
Capriciousness, Unreliable, Whimsical

Carnation, Red
Admiration, Ardor, Flashy, Passion, Pure love, Betrothal, Deep pure love, Fascination

Carnation, Striped
Indecision, Refusal, Rejection, Sorry I can't be with you

Carnation, White
Democracy, Devotion, Endearment, I am still available, Innocence, Living for love, Lovely, Pure and ardent love, Purity, Remembrance, Sweetness

Carnation, Yellow
Cheerful, Contempt, Disappointment, Disdain, No,
Rejection, Rue, Admiration, Fascination, I do not believe you,
You have disappointed me

Carob
Health, Protection

Carrot
Fertility, Lust

Cascara
Legal matters, Money, Protection

Cashew Nut
Money

Castor
Protection

Catalpa Tree
Beware of the Coquette

Catchfly
Pretend to Love, Snare, Unchanging Friendship, Youth

Catchfly, Red
I fall into a trap laid for me, Youthful Love

Catchfly, White
Betrayed

Catherine Wheel
Glory, Splendor

Catnip
Beauty, Cat Magic, Happiness, Love

Cattail
Lust, Peace, Prosperity

Cattleya
Matronly Grace, Mature Charm

Cedar Tree
Constancy in Love, Healing, I live but for thee, Incorruptible
Money, Protection, Purification, Strength, Think of me

Celandine
Happiness, Education, Escape, Future Joy, Joys to come,
Legal Matters, Protection

Celery
Lust, Mental powers, Psychic powers

Celosia
Affection, Singularity

Centaurea / Century Plant
Delicacy, Snake Removing, Delicate

Cereus, Creeping
Modest Genius

Cereus, Night-Blooming
Transient Beauty

Chamomile
Action, Comfort, Emotional Balance, Energy in Adversity,
Fortitude, Help against Wearisomeness, Logical Functioning,

Love, Meditation, Money, Patience, Physician Plant,
Purification, Sleep, Serenity, Sunny Disposition

Chaste Bush
Coldness, Indifference

Chaste Tree
Fertility, Purity

Cherry
Chivalry, Divination, Good Education, Good Works,
Insincerity, Love, Nobility, Sweetness of Character

Cherry Blossom
Beauty, Education, Kindness, Learning, Spiritual beauty,
Spirituality

Cherry Tree
Deception, Duration, Good education

Cherry Tree, White
Deception

Chervil
Sincerity

Chestnut
Affluence, Do me justice

Chestnut, Horse
Luxury

Chestnut Tree
Do me justice, Luxury

Chicory
Economy, Frugality

Chickweed
Assignation, Favors, Fertility, Frigidity, Give an account of yourself, I cling to you, Ingenious Simplicity, Invisibility, Love, Rendezvous, Removing Obstacles

Chili Pepper
Fidelity, Love

Chinaberry
Love, Death

Cinchona
Protection

Chinese Bellflower
Honesty, Obedience, Unchanging love

Chinese Ground Orchid
Beauty

Christmas Rose
Relieve my anxiety, Anxiety Relief

Chives
Strength, Protection

Chrysanthemum (Mum, Bloom)
Abundance, Cheerfulness, Cheerfulness in Old Age, Desolate Heart, Friendship, Innocence, Joy, Joviality, Innocence, Long Life, Loyal Love, Mirth, Optimism, Protection, Restfulness, Riches, Wealth, With Love, You are a Wonderful Friend

Chrysanthemum, Bronze
Excitement, Trust me

Chrysanthemum, Chinese
Cheerfulness under Adversity

Chrysanthemum, Red
I love you, I love you too

Chrysanthemum, White
Trust, Truth

Chrysanthemum, Yellow
Cheerfulness, Dejection, Secret admirer, Slighted, Slighted love

Cicely
Gladness, Sincerity, Rejoices and Comforts the Heart

Cilantro (Coriander)
Hidden worth

Cinchona
Luck, Delightful

Cinnamon
Beauty, Forgiveness of Injuries, Healing, Love, Lust Protection, My Fortune is Yours, Power, Psychic Powers, Spirituality

Cinquefoil
Beloved Daughter, Cherished, Maternal Affection, Money, Prophetic Dreams, Protection, Sleep

Citron
Ill-natured Beauty, Natural beauty, Psychic Powers, Sadness,
Sorrow

Clematis
Art, Artifice, Creativity, Filial love, I love your mind,
Ingenuity, Intelligence, Love from a Son or Daughter, Mental
Beauty, Unchanged for Eternity

Clematis, Evergreen
Poverty

Cleome
Elope with Me

Clianthus
Self-seeking, Worldliness

Climbing Lily
Fame, Honor

Cloth of Gold
Understanding animal languages

Clove
Love, Money, Protection

Clover
Education, Good Luck, Hard Work, Industry, Love, Money,
Protection, Revenge, Success

Clover, Four-Leaf
Be mine, Luck

Clover, Red
Building, Diligence, Industrious, Technology, Work

Clover, Three Leaf
Trinity

Clover, White
I promise, Luck, Remembrance, Think of me,

Cloves
Dignity, Nobility

Club Moss
Power, Protection

Cobaea
Gossip

Cohosh, Black
Courage, Love, Potency, Protection

Coconut
Chastity, Protection, Purification

Colchicum
Memories, Regret

Coleus
Heaven, Sky

Coltbur
Rudeness

Coltsfoot
Justice, Justice shall be done, Love, Visions

Columbine
Courage, Desertion, Energy, Folly, Foolishness, Gifts of the
Holy Spirit, Frivolous, Healing, I cannot give thee up,
Inconstancy, Inspiration, Love, Resolved to Win, Warrior
Spirit

Columbine, Purple
Resolved to win

Columbine, Red
Anxious, Trembling, Worried

Comfrey
Home sweet home, Money, Safety during Travel

Compass Flower
Faith

Coneflower
Capability, Healing, Immunity, Strength, Skill

Convolvulus (Bindweed, Morning Glory)
Bonds, Quandary, Uncertainty

Convolvulus, Pink
Worth sustained by judicious affection

Copal
Love, Purification

Coppertip
Wishes come true

Coral Bells
Challenge, Dainty Pleasures, Hard Work, Protection,
Scholarship

Corchorus
Impatience, Impatience of Absence, Return quickly

Coreopsis
Always cheerful, Cheerful, Happiness, Joy

Coreopsis, Arkansas
Love at first sight

Coriander (Cilantro)
Concealed merit, Healing, Health, Hidden worth, Love,
Never judge solely on appearances

Corn
Abundance, Divination, Luck, Protection, Riches, Gift of
Mother Nature

Corn Blossom
Riches

Corn Cockle
Peerless, Proud

Corn Straw
Agreement

Corn Straw, Broken
Quarrel

Cornet
Durability

Cornflower / Bachelor's Button
Blessings of being single, Celibacy, Daintiness, Delicacy,
Felicity, Healing, Independence, Refinement, Solitude

Cornella
Success will crown your riches, Success

Cosmos
Peace, Modesty, Pure love

Cotton
Fish Magic, Healing, Luck, Protection, Rain

Cotton Weed
Always remembered

Cowslip
Comeliness, Divine beauty, Divinity, Grace, Healing,
Pensiveness, Treasure finding, You are my divinity, You are
wonderful, Youth

Coxcomb
Affection, Conceited, Confidence, Faithful love, Foppery,
Humor, Pretension, Self-esteem, Singularity, Stillness

Crabapple Blossom
Irritability

Cranberry
Cure for heartache, Hardiness

Crane Flower
Faithfulness

Cranesbill (Geranium)
Envy, Consolation, Courtliness, Elegance, Folly, Friendship,
Gentility, Peace, I prefer you, Ingenuity, Silliness, Stupidity

Cranesbill, Dark
Melancholy

Cranesbill, Lemon
Unexpected meeting

Creeping Jennie / Lysimachia
Forgiveness

Creeping Lily
Fame, Honor

Crepe Myrtle
Love, Eloquence

Crepis, Bearded
Protection

Cress
Abuse not, Always reliable, Power, Stability

Crocosmia
Wishes come true

Crocus
Attachment, Cheerfulness, Exuberance, Foresight, Gladness,
Jovial, Joy, Mirth, Pleasure of hope, Visions, Youthful
Gladness

Crocus, Autumn
My best days are past

Crocus, Saffron
Mirth

Crocus, Spring
Youthful Gladness

Croton
Faithful

Crowsfoot
Ingratitude, Luster

Crown Imperial
Arrogance, Majesty, Power, Pride of Birth

Crown Vetch
Success, Success to you,

Cuckoo Flower
Adour, Acceptance, Fertility, Grounding, Lover, Protection, Tolerance

Cucumber
Chastity, Criticism, Fertility, Healing

Cudweed
Unceasing Remembrance

Cumin
Happiness, Peace, Protection

Cup and Saucer
Gossip

Cupid's Bower
Suffers from cold

Currant
Heals Conflicts, Joy, Peace, Relaxation, Serenity, Your Frown
Will Destroy Me, You Please All

Curry
Protection

Cuscuta
Meanness

Cushion Spurge
Persistence

Cyclamen
Diffidence, Endings, Farewell, Fertility, Good-bye,
Happiness, Lust, Modesty, Protection, Resignation, I
understand you

Cyclamen, Red
I will not economize

Cyclamen, White
Warmhearted

Cypress / Cypress Tree
Death, Deceitful, Despair, Healing, Longevity, Mourning,
Protection, Regard, Unrequited love, Vanity

Daffodil
Chivalry, Egotism, Esteem, Fertility, Gracefulness, Inner Self,
Love, Luck, Meditation, Regard, Respect, Self-Love, The Sun
Is Always Shining When I'm With You, Unrequited Love,
You're the Only One

Daffodil, Yellow
Gallantry

Dahlia
Capriciousness, Dignity, Elegance, Faithfulness, Forever Thine, Good Taste, Gratitude, Instability, Misrepresentation, My Gratitude Exceeds Your Care, Novelty, Pomp

Dahlia, Double
Participation

Dahlia, Single
Good taste

Dahlia, Variegated
I think of you constantly

Dahlia, White
Gratitude to parents

Dahlia, Yellow
Distaste, Rebuff

Daisy
Cheerfulness, Faithfulness, Finding Your Way, Intellect, I Will Think About it, Innocence, Loyal Love, Loyalty, Luck, Lust, Purity, Simplicity, Trust, Youthful Beauty

Daisy, Double
Enjoyment

Daisy, English
Cheerfulness, Innocence, I share your sentiments, Newborn Baby, Popular Oracle, Simplicity

Daisy, Garden
I share your sentiments

Daisy, Gerbera
Beauty, Thoughts of absent friends

Daisy, Michaelmas
Farewell

Daisy, Multi-colored
Beauty

Daisy, Ox-Eye
Token of affection, Patience

Daisy, Red
Beauty Unknown to Possessor

Daisy, White
Innocence

Daisy, Wild
I will think about it, Melancholy

Daisy, Wreath
I will think about it

Dame's Gillyflower / Dame's Rocket / Dame's Violet/ Dame's Wort
Coquetry, Evening, Virtue

Dandelion
Calling Spirits, Coquetry, Divination, Energy, Faithfulness, Flirting, Happiness, Lover's Oracle, Prophesy, Stress Release, Wishes

Daphne
Tolerance, Fame, Glory, Sweets to the sweet

Daphne Odora
Desire to Please, Sweetness

Darnel
Vice

Dates
Fertility, Potency

Datura
Deceit, Deceitful Charms, Protection, Separation, Sleep

Day Lily
Breaking up, Coquetry, Enthusiasm, Flirting, Loss of what could have been, Motherhood

Dead Leaves
Sadness, Sorrow

Deerstongue
Lust, Protection

Delphinium
Airy, Ardent Attachment, Beauty, Boldness, Fickleness, Flights of fancy, Fun, Gaiety, Haughtiness, Humor, Inner beauty, Magnanimous, Playfulness, Return of a Friend is Desired, Sweetness of Character, Well- Being

Devil's Bit
Love, Lust, Protection

Devil's Cucumber
Deceit

Devil's Shoestring
Gambling, Luck, Power, Protection

Devil's Trumpet
Deceit

Dew Plant
Serenade

Dianthus
Admiration, Beauty, Boldness, Chivalry, Devotion, Faithfulness, Fascination, Finesse, Gallantry, Grant me a smile, Make haste, My heart aches for you, Perfection, Pride, Pure and Deep Love, Scorn, Woman's Love

Dianthus, White
Talent

Digitalis
Healing, Charm

Dill
Luck, Lust, Money, Protection, Irresistible, Soothing

Diosma
Charm, Elegance, Your simple elegance charms me

Dittany of Crete
Astral Projection, Birth, Divination, Manifestations, Passion, Birth

Dock
Endurance, Fertility, Healing, Money, Patience

Dodder
Baseness, Divination, Knot Magic, Love

Dodder of Thyme
Baseness, Meanness

Dog Fennel
Action, Energy

Dog Rose
Pleasure and Pain

Dogsbane
Divination, Falsehood, Figment, I doubt you, Deception,
Durability

Dogwood Tree
Constancy, Crucifixion, Faithfulness, Indifferent, Love
Undiminished, Protection, Steadfastness, Success, Wishes

Dracaena
Inner power

Dragon Plant
Dread, Snare

Dragon Root
Adour

Dragon's Blood
Love, Potency, Protection

Dragon's Wort
Astonishment, Horror

Dusty Miller
Felicity, Delicacy, Happiness, Industriousness,
Venerable

Dutchman's Britches
Elegance, Fidelity, Love, Love Attraction

Ebony
Power, Protection

Echinacea
Strengthening

Echites
Be warned in time

Edelweiss
Courage, Invisibility, Nobility, Purity

Eglantine
Genius, I wound to heal, Poetry, Talent

Elder
Compassion, Humiliation, Protection, Psychic powers,
Regret, Zealousness

Elderberry
Kindness, Compassion, Zeal

Elecampane
Creativity, Emotional Stability, Love, Protection, Psychic
Powers

Elm Tree
Dignity, Love, Majesty, Patriotism

Endive
Frugality, Love, Lust, Money Management

Eryngo
Peace, Lust, Love, Travelers' Luck

Eucalyptus
Healing, Protection

Euonymus / Spindle Tree
Long Life, Your image is engraved on my heart

Eupatorium
Delay

Euphorbia
Persistence, Protection, Purification

Eustoma
Beautiful mouth, Optimistic, Outgoing, Playful, Well spoken

Evergreen
Indigence

Everlasting
Always Remembered, Cheerfulness under adversity, Eternity,
I think of thee, Immortality, Memories, Never-ceasing
remembrance, Remembrance

Everlasting Pea
Bliss, Blissful pleasure, Chastity, Courage, Delicate Pleasures,
Departure, Friendship, Good-bye, Let's meet, Remember me,
Shyness, Strength, Tenderness, Thank you for a good time

Eyebright
Cheer up, Mental Powers, Psychic powers

Fair Lily
Fond Caresses, Love, Sincerity

Falling Start
Wishes come true

False Goat's Beard
I'll still be waiting

Fennel
Courage, Flattery and Deceit, Force, Hardness, Healing, Protection, Purification, Strength, Thinness

Fenugreek
Money

Fern
Allure, Confidence, Eternal Youth, Fascination, Healing, Health, Luck, Magic, Protection, Rain, Rain Making, Riches, Shelter, Sincerity

Fern, Asparagus
Grace

Fern, Flowering
Reverie

Fern, Maidenhair
Beauty, Discretion, Love, Secrecy, Secret bond of love

Fern, Male
Love, Luck

Fern, Walking
Mobility

Feverfew
Protection, Good health, Warmth, You light up my life, Flirt

Fig
Argument, Divination, Fertility, I keep my secret, Longevity, Love, Fecundity, Peace and Prosperity

Fig Marigold
Coldness

Fig Tree
Prolific

Figwort
Future joy, Health, Protection

Filbert Nut
Reconciliation

Fir Tree
Awe, Elation, Elevation, Enthusiasm, Holiness, Protection, Time, Wonder

Fire Lily
Fame, Honor

Fireball Lily
Glory, Splendor

Flags (Iris)
Eloquence, Faith, Hope, Message, Missive, My compliments, Valor Wisdom, Your friendship is valued

Flame Lily
Fame, Honor

Flamingo Flower
Graciousness

Flax
Beauty, Benefactor, Benevolence, Domestic happiness, Fate, Healing, I feel your kindness, Money, Protection, Psychic Powers

Flax, Dried
Industry, Utility

Fleabane
Chastity, Protection, Thank you

Fleur de Lis (Iris)
Ardor, Flame, Eloquence, Message, My Compliments, Promise of Good Things to Come

Florist's Nightmare
Atonement, Hope, Idleness, Purity, Reconciliation

Floss Flower
Longevity

Flower of an Hour
Delicate beauty

Foam Flower
Attractive

Forget-Me-Not
Constancy, Do Not Forget Me, Dreams, Hope, Memories, Personal Relationships, Release of Negativity, Remembrance, True Love Forever

Forsythia
Anticipation, Good nature

Fountain Plant
Hopelessness

For O'clock / Marvel of Peru
Shyness, Timidity, Wonderful

Foxglove
Decision, Hypocrisy, Insincerity, Protection, Stateliness,
Wish, You are false, Youth

Foxtail
Sporting

Frankincense (Boswellia)
Faithful Heart, Exorcism, Protection, Spirituality

Fraxinella
Fire

Freesia
Friendship, Innocence, Spirited, Trust

French Buttercup
Charm

Friar's Cap
Warning

Fritillaria
Majesty

Frog Lily
Disgust

Fuchsia
Ambition of my Love Plagues Itself, Amiability, Confiding Love, Frugality, Good Taste, Humble Love, Taste

Fumitory
Exorcism, Hatred, Money

Fungus
Disgust, Loneliness, Resilience, Solitude

Furze
Anger, General love

Fuzzy Weed
Hunting, Love

Galax/Wandflower
Encouragement, Friendship

Gaillardia
Joy

Gardenia
Ecstasy, Feminine Charm, Healing, I Love You In Secret, Joy, Love, Loveliness, Peace, Peace and Prosperity, Refinement, Secret Love, Spirituality, Transport of Joy, You Are Lovely

Garlic
Anti-theft, Courage, Healing, Lust, Protection, Strength, Good Luck

Gay Feather
Enthusiasm, I'll try again

Gentian
Dreams, Integrity, Love, Power, Prayer, Self-esteem, You are
unfair, Self-communication, Perception of reality, Healing of
the spirit, Loveliness, Righteousness, You are unjust

Gentian, Closed
Sweet Dreams

Gentian, Yellow
Ingratitude

Geranium
Childishness, Comfort, Conjugal Affection, Courtliness,
Deceit, Elegance, Esteem, Fertility, Folly, Friendship,
Gentility, Health, Ingenuity, I Prefer You, Love, Melancholy,
Protection, Silliness, Stupidity

Geranium, Apple
Facility, Present Preference

Geranium, Dark
Melancholy, Your looks freeze me

Geranium, Fish
Disappointed expectation

Geranium, Ivy
Bridal Favor, Your hand for the next dance

Geranium, Lemon
Unexpected Meeting

Geranium, Nutmeg
Expected meeting

Geranium, Oak-leaf
True Friendship

Geranium, Penciled
Ingenuity

Geranium, Rose-scented
Preference

Geranium, Scarlet
Comfort, Stupidity

Geranium, Silver
Recall

Geranium, White
Gracefulness

Geranium, Wild
Availability, Constancy, Envy, I desire to please, Steadfastness

Gerbera Daisy
Friendship, Innocence, Needing protection, Sadness

Gillyflower
Bonds of affection, Enduring Beauty, Faithfulness, Lasting Beauty, Promptness, Thou art fair

Ginger
Comforting , Love, Money, Power, Pride, Success, Safe, Pleasant, Warming

Ginger, Blue
Health, Lust, Money, Protection, Psychic powers

Ginseng
Beauty, Healing, Love, Lust, Protection, Wishes

Gladiolus (Glads)
Character, Flower of the Gladiators, Generosity, Give me a break, I'm really sincere, Love at first sight, Natural grace, Ready-armed, Sincerity, Strength of character, You Pierce my Heart

Glasswort
Pretension

Globe Amaranth
Constant, Immortality, Steadfast, Unchangeable, Unfading Love

Globe Flower / Trollius
Generosity, Gratitude, Solitude

Gloriosa Daisy
Impartiality

Glory Lily
Fame, Honor, Glorious Beauty

Gloxinia
Love at first sight

Goat's Rue
Healing, Health, Reason

Golden Chain Tree
Pensive Beauty

Golden Seal
Healing, Money

Goldenrod
Be cautious, Divination, Divine guidance, Encouragement, Good fortune, Money, Precaution, Support, Waning, You will succeed

Gooseberry
Anticipation, Ease, Enjoyment, Energy, Goodness, Peace, Protection

Gorse
Affection, Anger, Attraction, Endearing affection, Health, Ire, Love in all seasons, Lust, Money, Passion, Protection, Vitality

Gotu Kola
Meditation

Gourd
Bulk, Extent, Protection, Spirituality

Grain
Protection, Plenty

Grains of Paradise
Love, Luck, Lust, Money, Wishes

Grape
Abandonment, Carousing, Domestic Happiness, Garden Magic, Intoxication, Mental Powers, Money, Prosperity and Plenty

Grape Hyacinth
Encouragement, Romantic love, Unobtrusive Loveliness

Grape, Wild
Charity, Mirth

Grass
Fleeting Life, Protection, Psychic powers, Submission, Utility

Grass Pea
Bliss, Blissful pleasure, Chastity, Courage, Delicate pleasures, Departure, Friendship, Good-bye, Let's meet, Remember me, Shyness, Strength, Shyness, Tenderness, Thank you for a good time

Groundseal
Objectivity

Ground Ivy
Divination

Guelder Rose
Boredom, Bound, Ennui, Thoughts of heaven

Harebell
Grief, Pain, Submission

Harlequin Flower
Laugh at trouble

Hawkweed
Quick -sighted

Hawthorn
Chastity, Desire, Expectation, Fear, Fertility, Fishing magic, Funerals, Happiness, Hope, Luck in fishing , Obstacles, Protection for Ships, Shame

Hazel (Filbert)
Anti-lightening, Enlightenment, Fertility, Heart is agitated, Inspiration, Knowledge, Luck, Peace, Protection, Reconciliation, Reunion, Wisdom, Wishes

Heartsease / Johnny Jump Up
Happy Thoughts, Love in idleness, Modesty, Pleasant thoughts, Think of me, You occupy my thoughts

Heath
Solitude

Heather
Acceptance, Admiration, Courtship, Loneliness, Love, Lovers, Luck, Protection, Protection from Danger, Rain making, Solitude, Wishes will come true

Heather, Lavender
Admiration, Solitude

Heather, White
Good luck, Protection, Wishes

Hellebore
Anxiety Relief, Balance, Calumny, Goals, Malicious Representation, Poise, Relieve My Anxiety, Self-Assurance, Shyness Reduction, Slander, Tension Relief, You Have Listened to Scandal

Hellebore, Black
Protection

Helenium
Tears

Heliotrope
Attachment, Devotion, Eagerness, Eternal love, Faithfulness, Healing, I adore you, Intoxicated with joy, Invisibility, Let us pray for each other, Prophetic dreams, Wealth, Worship

Hemlock
Chastity, Triumph over winter, You will cause my death

Hemp
Fate, Healing, Love, Meditation, Visions

Henbane
Beware, Danger, Female Attraction

Henna
Healing

Hen and Chicks / Sedum
Motherly Love, Welcome home drunk husband

Hepatica
Confidence

Hibiscus
Delicate beauty, Divination, Love, Lust, Mildness, Passion, Sweet disposition

Hickory Tree
Legal Matters

High John the Conqueror
Happiness, Love, Money, Success

Holly
Am I forgotten?, Anti-lightening, Challenge, Defense,
Domestic Happiness, Dream magic, Enchantment, Far
Sightedness, Foresight, Good will, Good wishes, Lightening
Protection, Luck, Strengthening, Testing, Transformation,
Trials

Holly Berries
Christmas Joy, Protection

Hollyhock
Ambition, Ambition of a scholar, Aspiration, Fecundity,
Fertility, Fruitfulness, I will seek glory

Hollyhock, White
Female ambition

Honesty
Accepting change in life, Fascination, Flexibility,
Forgetfulness, Honesty, Money, Relationships, Self-
knowledge, Sincerity, Trustworthiness

Honey Flower
Sweet and secret love

Honeysuckle
Affection, Bonds of love, Devoted love, Do you love me?
Domestic happiness, Fidelity, Fraternal affection, Generosity,
Generous and devoted love, Happiness, Love, Money,
Protection, Psychic Powers, Sweet disposition, Wedding will
follow shortly

Hops
Healing, Injustice, Mirth, Rest, Sleep

Horehound
Fire, Healing, Mental Powers, Protection

Hornbeam
Ornament

Horse Chestnut Tree
Healing, Luxury, Money

Horseradish
Purification

Horsetail
Fertility

Hosta
Devotion

House Leek
Domestic industry, Love, Luck, Protection, Vivacity

Houstonia
Contentment, Innocence

Hoya
Art, Sculpture

Huckleberry
Dream magic, Faith, Luck, Protection, Simple pleasures

Humble Plant
Bashfulness, Sensibility

Hurtsickle
Anticipation, Blessings of being single, Celibacy,
Independence, Solitude

Hyacinth
Constancy, Dedication, Games, Happiness, Impulsiveness,
Love, Playfulness, Protection, Rashness, Sincerity, Sorrow,
Sports

Hyacinth, Blue
Consistency, Constancy

Hyacinth, Purple
Apology, Grief, I'm sorry, Jealousy, Please forgive me,
Sadness, Sorrow

Hyacinth, Red or Pink
Joy, Playfulness

Hyacinth, White
Beauty, I'll pray for you, Prayer, Unobtrusive loveliness

Hyacinth, Wild
Mysterious, Viligance

Hyacinth, Yellow
Jealousy

Hydrangea
Boaster, Braggart, , Devotion, Frigidity, Heartlessness,
Perseverance, Understanding, You are cold

Hypericum
Protection, Superstition, You are a prophet

Hyssop
Protection, Purification, Cleanliness

Ice Plant
Old beau, Rejected, Rejected suitor, Your looks freeze me

Iceland Moss
Health

Impatiens
Ardent Love, Felicity, Impatience, Motherly Love

Indian Paintbrush
Love

Ipomoea
Attachment

Iris
Eloquence, Faith, Friendship, Hope, Inspiration, I have a message for you, Missive, My compliments, Passion, Promise, Purification, Valor, Wisdom, Your friendship is valued

Iris, Bearded
Ardor

Iris, Blue
Money

Iris, German
Aflame, I burn

Iris, Yellow
Passion, Sorrow

Irish Moss
Luck, Money, Protection

Ismene
Elope with me, I'm not so bad as I seem

Italian Cypress
Death

Ivy
Achievement, Affection, Ambition, Conjugal affection,
Constancy, Fealty, Fidelity, Friendship, Growth, Healing,
Loyalty, Marriage, Protection, Tenacity, Trustfulness, Wedded
Love

Jacob's Ladder
Come down to me

Japanese Rose
Beauty is your only attraction

Japonica
Love, Perfection, Sincerity, Unpretending Excellence

Japonica, Pyrus
Fairies' fire

Jasmine
Amiability, Attachment, Congeniality, Elegance, Grace, Love,
Modesty, Money, Prophetic Dreams, Sensuality, Transport of
joy

Jasmine, Carolina
Amiability, Elegance, Gracefulness, Separation

Jasmine, Spanish
Sensuality

Jasmine, White
Amiability

Jasmine, Yellow
Elegance, Grace

Jersey Lily
Prosperity

Jewel Weed
Deceit, Impatience, Motherly love

Job's Tears
Good luck, Healing, Luck, Wishes

Joe Pye Weed
Delay, Love, Respect

Johnny Jump- Up / Heartsease
In my thoughts, Happy Thoughts

Jonquil
Affection, Affection returned, Chivalry, Desire, Have pity on my passion, , I desire a return of affection, Love, Regard, Respect, Sympathy, Unrequited love

Joseph's Coat
Hopelessness

Judas Tree
Betrayal

Juniper
Anti-theft, Asylum, Exorcism, Health, Helpfulness, Love, Protection, Protection from Snakes, Succor, Welcome to new home

Jupiter's Beard
Love, Protection, Purity
Kalanchoe
Popularity

Kale, Flowering
Money

Kansas Feather
Enthusiasm, I'll try again

Kava-Kava
Luck, Protection, Visions

Kennedia
Intelligence, Mental beauty

Keys of Heaven
Love, Protection, Purity

Kill Weed
Sports

Kingscup
Desire for riches, I wish I was rich

Kiss Me Over The Garden Gate
I blush for you

Kalanchoe
Popularity

Knotweed
Binding, Health, Restoration

Kudzu
Don't stand still, Live life in the fast lane, Stay out of my way

Laburnum
Pensive Beauty

Lady's Mantle
Attract love, Love

Lady's Seal
Capriciousness, Catch me if you can, Helpfulness, Protection, Support

Lady's Slipper
Capricious Beauty, Fickleness

Lady's Thumb
I blush for you

Lamb's Ears
Support, Softness, Gentleness, Surprise, Support

Lancaster Rose
Agreement

Lantana
Rigor

Larch Tree
Anti-theft, Audacity, Boldness, Protection

Larkspur
Airy, Ardent Attachment, Fickleness, Flights of fancy, Fun, Gaiety, Health, Humor, Inner Beauty, Levity, Lightness, Open heart, Protection, Swiftness

Larkspur, Pink
Fickleness

Laurel Tree (Sweet Bay, Bay)
Accomplishment, Achievement in the arts, Civil Service, Courage, Creation of Beauty, Glory, Perfidy, Personal Achievement, Reward of merit, Sharpness, Success

Lauresina
I die if neglected

Laurustinus
Cheerful

Lavatera
Delicate Beauty, Sweetness

Lavender
Acknowledgment, Ardent Attachment, Blocks Emotional Conflicts, Chastity, Devotion, Distrust, Failure, Happiness, I Like You Only As A Friend, Longevity, Love, Luck, Peace, Protection, Purification, Refusal, Sleep, Soothes, the Heart, Suspicion, Sensitivity, Success

Leadwort
Success, Sympathy

Leek
Exorcism, Love, Protection

Lemon
Discretion, Fidelity in love, Friendship, Longevity, Love, Purification, Zest

Lemon Blossom
Discretion, Faithfulness, Fidelity

Lemon Grass
Lust, Psychic Powers, Snake repelling

Lemon Verbena
Love, Purification

Lenten Rose
Anxiety Relief, Calumny, Malicious Representation, Relieve my anxiety, Slander, Wit, You have listened to scandal

Lettuce
Chastity, Cold-hearted, Divination, Love, Protection, Sleep

Lichen
Dejection, Hanging on to old ways, Solitude

Licorice
Fidelity, Love, Lust

Lilac
Acceptance, Beauty, Do You Still Love Me? Fastidiousness, First Love, Fraternal Regard, Love, Modesty, Pride, Purity, Youth

Lilac, Field
Humility

Lilac, Purple
First emotions of love

Lilac, White
Youthful innocence

Lily
Beauty, Breaking up, Coquetry, Elegance, Enthusiasm,
Honor, Innocence, Motherhood, Nobility, Pride, Purity,
Sweetness

Lily of the Incas
Prosperity

Lily of the Nile
Retirement happiness, Love letters

Lily of the Valley
Return of happiness, You've made my life complete,
Happiness, Humility, Mental ability, Purity, Sweetness

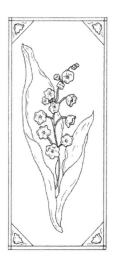

Lily, Day
Flirting, Mother

Lily, Eucharis
Charm

Lily, Foxtail
Aspiration

Lily, Scarlet
High of soul

Lily, Frog
Disgust

Lily, Orange
Enemy, Hatred, Passion

Lily, Purple
First love

Lily, Tiger
Fun, I dare you to love me, Riches

Lily, White
Beauty, Modesty, Purity, Sweetness

Lily, Yellow
Coquetry, Falsehood, Flirtation, Gaiety, Happiness, Lies

Lime
Marital Affection

Lime Tree
Conjugal attraction, Marriage

Linaria
Deception

Linden Tree
Judgments, Lenient, Prophecies, Yielding

Lisanthus
Beautiful Mouth, Calmness, Optimistic, Outgoing, Playful, Showy, Well -Spoken

Liverwort
Confidence, Love, Protection

Lobelia
Arrogance, Malevolence

Lobelia, Scarlet
Distinction, Honor

Locust Tree
Affection beyond the grave, Elegance

London Pride
Look up and Kiss me, Whimsy

Long Purples
Sporting

Loosestrife
Forgiveness, Peace, Pretension, Protection, Wishes Granted

Lotus
Birth, Enlightenment, Estranged Love, Fertility, Protection

Lotus Leaf
Recantation

Lovage
Love, Strength

Love in a Mist / Nigella
Calmness, Delicacy, Embarrassment, Independence, Kiss me twice before I rise, Love, Motivation, Perplexity, Prosperity and Plenty, Questioning

Love in a Puzzle
Embarrassment

Love Lies Bleeding/Amaranthus
Heartless, Hopeless, Hopelessness

Love Seed
Friendship, Love

Lucerne
Life

Lucky Hand
Employment, Friendship, Luck, Money, Protection, Travel

Lungwort
Life

Lupine
Dejection, Imagination, Voraciousness

Lupine, Rose
Fanciful

Lupine, White
Happy always

Lychnis
Religion, Religious Enthusiasm, Wit

Mace
Mental Powers, Psychic Powers, Understanding

Madder
Calumny, Scandal, Tranquility

Madrone
Faithfulness, One love

Magic Flower
Suffer from cold

Magic Lily
Dance with me

Magnolia
Dignity, Fidelity, Nature, Nobility, Perseverance, Sweetness, Beauty, Love of nature

Maguey
Lust

Mahogany
Anti-lightening

Marjoram
Blushes, Happiness, Health, Humor, Illusion, Love, Money, Protection

Mallow
Consumed by love, Delicate Beauty, Love, Mildness,
Protection, Passion, Sweetness

Maltese Cross
Dance with me, Religion

Manchineel
Betrayal, Falsehood, Little apple of death

Mandevilla
Reckless, Thoughtless

Mandrake
Fertility, Health, Honor, Love, Money, Protection, Rarity

Maple Tree
Beauty, Elegance, Keys, Longevity, Love, Money, Reserve

Maple Tree, Japanese
Baby's hands, Poetry (especially Haiku)

Marguerite
Action, Energy

Marigold
Chagrin, Cruelty, Cruelty in love, Despair, Despondency,
Grief, Hearth's comfort, I have cause, Inquietude, Jealousy,
Legal matters, Prophetic dreams, Protection, Psychic powers,
Riches, Sacred Affection, Trouble, Uneasiness

Marigold, African
Vulgar minds

Marigold, Cape
Omen, Presage

Marigold, French
Jealousy

Marigold, Garden
Trouble

Marigold, Pot / Calendula
Health, Joy, Remembrance

Marigold with Red Flowers
The varying course of life

Marjoram
Delusion

Marsh Mallow
Beneficence, Healing, Honesty, Persuasion, Purity

Marvel of Peru
Timidity, Wonderful

Marsh Rosemary
Success, Sympathy

Masterwort
Courage, Protection, Strength

Mastic
Lust, Manifestations, Psychic Powers

May Apple
Money

Mayflower
Budding beauty, Coming of age

May Weed
Action, Energy

Meadow Saffron
Cherished, Domestic Duties, Domestic Virtue, Esteem, Growing Old, Long Life, Memories, Past, Regret, Wisdom

Meadow Sage
Cherished, Domestic duties, Domestic virtue, Esteem, Long life, Wisdom

Meadowsweet
Divination, Happiness, Love, Peace, Uselessness

Melissa
Fellowship, Joke, Sympathy

Mesquite
Healing

Mezereon
Flirt, Desire to please

Michaelmas Daisy
Afterthought, Daintiness, Farewell, Love, Variety

Mignonette
Healing, I live for thee, Your qualities surpass your charms

Milfoil
War

Milk Vetch
Soothing, Your presences softens my pains

Milkwort
Hermitage

Mimosa Tree
Do not hurt me, Love, Modesty, Prophetic dreams,
Protection, Purification, Secret Love, Sensitive, Sensibility

Mint
Healing, Love, Lust, Money, Protection, Travel, Virtue

Mission Bells
Persecution

Mistletoe (Heal All)
Balance, Creativity, Fertility, Health, Holiness, Kiss Me, Love,
Obstacles, Overcome Difficulties, Peace, Protection, Sense of
Self, Warding, Welcome

Mock Orange
Counterfeit, Deceit, Uncertainty

Molukka Bean
Protection

Monarda
Your whims are unbearable

Money Plant
Fascination, Forgetfulness, Honesty, Sincerity

Monk's Head
Elegance, Fidelity, Love Attraction

Monkshood
A foe is near, Chivalry, Deadly foe is near, Deception, Warning

Montbretia
Wishes come true

Moon Vine / Moonflower
Attachment, Breath of an angel, I only dream of thee, Instability, Night

Moonwort
Forgetfulness, Love, Money

Morning Glory
Affection, Coquetry, Dead hope, Departure, Extinguished hope, I love you, Insincerity, Transience

Morning Glory, Dwarf
Bonds

Morning Glory, Red
Attachment

Moschatel
Weak but winning

Moss
Ennui, Luck, Maternal love, Money

Moss Rose
Voluptuousness

Moss Rosebud
Confessed love, Confession of love

Mossy Saxifrage
Affection

Mother of the Evening
Coquetry, Evening, Virtue

Motherwort
Concealed love, Secret love

Mountain Ash Tree
Prudence

Mountain Laurel
Ambition, Ambition of a hero, Treachery, Victory

Mouse Ear
Do not forget me

Mudwort
Tranquility

Mugwort
Absence, Astral Projection, , Conception, Encouragement,
Good luck, Happiness, Healing, Prophetic dreams,
Protection, Psychic powers, Strength, Tranquility

Mulberry
Protection, Strength

Mulberry, White
Wisdom

Mullein
Courage, Divination, Good natured, Health, Love,
Protection, Self-knowledge, Self-empowerment,
Communication

Mum
Abundance, Cheerfulness, Riches, Wealth, You are a
wonderful friend

Mum, Red
I Love You

Mum, Yellow
Slighted love

Mushroom
Suspicion

Musk Plant
Weakness

Muskmallow
Delicate beauty, Sweetness

Mustard
Fertility, Indifference, Mental Powers, Protection

Mustard Seed
Faith, Indifference

Myosotis
Forget me not

Myrobalan
Privation

Myrrh
Gladness, Healing, Protection, Spirituality

Myrtle
Joy, Love

Myrtle, Wax
Discipline, Instruction

Naked Lady
Drama, Dance with me

Narcissus
Egotism, Formality, Selfishness, Stay as sweet as you are, Uncertainty, You love yourself too much

Nasturtium
Charity, Conquest, Maternal love, Patriotism, Victory, Victory in battle

Nettle
Concert, Cruelty, Emotional calmness, Healing, Lust, Protection, Stress relief, Sibling relationships

Nicotiana
Cleansing

Night Scented Gillyflower
Coquetry, Evening, Virtue

Nightshade
Bitter truth, Dark thoughts, Falsehood, Silence, Sorcery, Truth, Verity, Your thoughts are dark

Nosegay
Gallantry

Nuts
Fertility, Love, Luck, Prosperity

Oak Leaf
Strength

Oak, Live
Liberty

Oak Sprig
Hospitality

Oak Tree
Endurance, Hospitality, Maturity, Progress, Protection, Strength

Oats
Money, Music

Oenothera
Unfaithful

Oleander
Beware, Caution

Olive Tree
Beneficence, Fertility, Lust, Peace, Peace and Victory, Potency, Protection, Studious pursuit

Olive, Russian
Bitterness

Onion
Healing, Lust, Money, Prophetic dreams, Protection

Ophrys, Frog
Disgust

Orange
Love, Luck, Money

Orange Blossom
Eternal love, Fertility, Innocence, Love, Luck, Marriage, Money

Orange Flower
Bridal festivities, Chastity

Orchid
Adroitness, Beautiful lady, Beauty, Belle, Delicate beauty, Error, Long life, Love, Magnificence, Many children, Rare beauty, Refinement, Thoughtfulness, You flatter me, I await your pleasures

Orchid, Cattleya
Mature charm

Orchid, Cymbidium
Beauty, Love, Luxury, Magnificence, Scholarship

Orchid, Spider
Skill

Oregano
Birth, Peace

Oregon Grape
Money, Prosperity

Orris
Divination, Love, Protection

Osier
Frankness

Osmunda
Dreams, I dream of you, Reverie

Our Lady's Earrings
Impatience, Motherly love

Oxalis
Joy, Funny, Secret sweetness

Ox-Eye Daisy
Patience, Joy

Painted Daisy
Joy

Painter's Palette
Graciousness

Palm
Fertility, Potency, Success, Victory

Palm Leaves
Success, Victory

Pansy
Divination, Fun, Love, Intuition, Pleasant thoughts, Rain magic, Think of me, Thinking of you, Thoughts

Pansy, Frilled
Risque

Pansy, Purple
You occupy my thoughts

Pansy, Yellow and Purple
Forget me not

Papaya
Love, Protection

Papyrus
Protection

Parosela
Hunting

Parsley
Banquet, Entertainment, Feasting, Festivity, Gratitude, Joy,
Love, Protection, Purification, Thanks, Useful knowledge

Parsley and Rue Together
Beginnings

Pasque Flower
Belief, Faith, Friendship, Peach, Religion, Sleep
Unpretentious, You have no claims

Passion Flower
Compassion, Spirituality

Patchouli
Fertility, Lust, Money

Patient Lucy
Impatience, Motherly love

Pea
Love, Money, Departure, Happy marriage, Profits in business, Respect

Peach
Fertility, Longevity, Love, Submission, Wishes, I am your captive

Peach Blossom
My heart is thine

Pear
Affection, Love, Lust, Benevolent justice, Health, Good government, Wise administration

Pear Tree
Affection, Comfort

Pecan
Employment, Money

Pennyroyal
Flee away, Peace, Protection, Strength, Clarity of thought, Positive thoughts

Pentsemon
Creativity

Peony
Anger, Bashfulness, Bravery, Contrition, Hands Full of Cash, Happiness, Healing, Indignation, Marriage, Ostentation, Prosperity, Protection, Shame, Shyness

Pepper
Protection

Pepper Tree
Healing, Protection

Peppermint
Cordiality, Healing, Love, Psychic powers, Purification, Sleep, Warmth

Perilla
Role reversal

Periwinkle
Love, Lust, Memories, Mental powers, Money, Protection, Sweet remembrance

Periwinkle, Blue
Early attachment, Early friendship

Periwinkle, White
Pleasures of memory

Persian Buttercup
Charm, Attraction

Persian Violet
Diffidence, Fertility, Good-bye, Lust, Protection, Resignation

Persimmon
Bury me amid nature's beauties, Healing, Luck

Peruvian Daffodil
Elope with me, I'm not as bad as I seem

Peruvian Lily
Fortune, Money

Petunia
Anger, Never despairing, Not proud, Resentment, Your presence sooths me

Pheasant's Eye
Bitter memories, Painful remembrance, Sorrowful memories

Phlox
Agreement, Our hearts are united, Proposal of love, Souls united, Sweet dreams, Unanimity

Pilewort
Future joy

Pimento
Love

Pimpernel
Assignation, Change, Chosen One, Dreams, Harmony, Health, Protection, Rendezvous

Pincushion Flower
Unfortunate love

Pine
Fertility, Healing, Hope, Mobility, Money, Pity, Protection, Spiritual energy

Pine Cone
Fertility, Life

Pine Tree
Awe, Courage, Elation, Endurance, Enthusiasm, Wonder

Pine (Pitch Pine)
Philosophy

Pine (Umbrella Pine)
Honoring the dead, Joy, Respect, Undying love

Pineapple
Chastity, Hospitality, Luck, Money, Perfection, Welcome,
You are perfect

Pinks
Affection, Aversion, Boldness, Chivalry, Finesse, Gallantry,
Grant me a smile, Perfection, Pure affection, Scorn

Pistachio
Breaking up

Plantain
Adulation, Healing, Protection, Strength, Pilgrimage, Well-
trodden path

Plum
Healing, Promises

Plum Tree
Genius, Independence

Plumbago
Antidote, Holy wishes, Success, Sympathy

Plumeria
Love

Poinsettia
Celebration, Good cheer, Mirth, Success

Poison Root
Glory, Splendor

Poke / Poke Salat
Courage

Polonium
Breaking

Policeman's Helmet
Impatience, Motherly love

Pomegranate
Conceited, Divination, Elegance, Fertility, Luck, Wealth, Wishes

Poplar Tree
Flying, Money

Poplar Tree, Black
Courage

Poplar Tree, White
Time

Poppy
Consolation, Death, Dreaminess, Eternal Sleep, Evanscent Pleasure, Extravagance, Fertility, Imagination, Invisibility, Love, Luck, Money, Oblivion, Sleep

Poppy, California
Do not refuse me

Poppy, Red
Passion, Pleasure

Poppy, White
Consolation, Dormant affection, My bane and my antidote,
Sleep

Poppy, Yellow
Success, Wealth

Portulaca
It's time

Pot Marigold
Joy

Potato
Beneficence, Healing, Image magic

Prairie Gentian / Prairie Rose
Beautiful mouth, Optimistic, Outgoing, Playful, Well- spoken

Prayer Plant
Bashfulness, Sensibility

Pretty Face
Hope, Watchfulness

Prickly Pear
I burn

Prickly Burr
Deceit

Primrose
Comeliness, Divine beauty, Divinity, Grace, Healing Heart's
mystery, Love, Pensiveness, Protection, You are my divinity,
You are wonderful, Youth

Primrose, Evening
Unfaithful, Youth

Primrose, Yellow
Hunting

Prince of Wales Feather
Hopelessness

Prince's Feather
I blush for you

Privet Hedge
Prohibition

Pukeweed
Arrogance

Pumpkin
Coarseness

Purple Willow Herb/ Purple Grass
Sports

Purslane
Happiness, Love, Luck, Protection, Sleep

Pussy Willow
Mother, Recovery from illness

Quaking Grass
Agitation

Quamash
Mysterious

Queen Anne's Lace
Do not refuse me, Femininity, I'll return

Queen Anne's Thimbles
Enduring beauty, Promptness

Queen's Gillyflower
Coquetry, Evening, Virtue

Queen's Rocket
Fashion

Quince
Cheers my soul, Happiness, Love, Protection, Temptation,
Triteness

Radish
Lust, Protection

Ragweed
Courage, Love returned, Nuisance, Your love is returned

Rain Lily
Fond caresses, Love, Sincerity

Rainbow Weed
Sports

Ranunculus
Charm, Radiant

Raspberry
Fulfillment, Gentle-heartedness, Happiness, Love, Protection,
Remorse

Rattlesnake Root
Money, Protection

Red Cape Lily
Glory, Splendor

Red Hot Poker
Dangerous, Determined

Red Sally
Sports

Red Swallowwort
Let me go

Reed
Complaisance, Imprudence, Music, Prayer

Rhododendron
Agitation, Beware, Danger, Warning

Rhubarb
Brouhaha, Fidelity, Protection

Rice
Money, Fertility, Protection, Rain

Rogue's Gillyflower
Coquetry, Evening, Virtue

Roots
Divination, Power, Protection

Rose
Always, Desire, Divination, Friendship, Gladness, Happiness, Healing, I love you, Love, Love at first sight, Joy, Passion,

Perfect happiness, Please believe me, Psychic powers, Unity, Warmth of heart, You are everything to me

Rose Bouquet
Gratitude

Rose Champion
Dance with me

Rose Leaf
You may hope

Rose Mallow
Delicate beauty, Love, Mildness, Passion

Rose of Sharon
Consumed by love, Delicate Beauty, Firey love, Love, Mildness, Persuasion, Passion

Rose, Black
Death, Hatred, Obsession, Rebirth

Rose, Blue
Mystery, Wistfulness

Rose, Bridal
Happy love

Rose, Burgundy
Unconscious beauty

Rose, Cabbage
Ambassador of love

Rose, Carolina
Love is dangerous

Rose, Champion
You only deserve my love

Rose, China
Beauty always new

Rose, Coral
Desire, Enthusiasm

Rose, Crown or Garland
Reward of virtue

Rose, Daily
Thy smile I aspire to

Rose, Damask
Bashful love, Brilliant complexion, Youth

Rose, Dark Crimson
Mourning

Rose, Dark Red
Mourning

Rose, Deep Pink
Thank you

Rose, Deep Red
Bashful shame

Rose, Dog
Mixed Feelings, Pleasure and Pain

Rose, Dried White
Death preferable to loss of innocence

Rose, Eglantine
Poetry

Rose, Full Over Two Buds
Secrecy

Rose, Gold
Absolute achievement

Rose, Guelder
Age, Good news, Winter

Rose, Lavender
Enchantment, Love at first sight

Rose, Light Pint
Friendship

Rose, Long Stemmed
I will always remember you

Rose, Maiden Blush
If you love me, you will find it out

Rose, Multiflora
Grace, Gracefulness

Rose, Mundi
Variety, You are Merry

Rose, Musk
Capricious beauty

Rose, Orange
Desire, Enthusiasm, Fascination, Passionate interest

Rose, Peach
Desire, Enthusiasm, Shyness

Rose, Pink
Friendship, Perfect happiness, Please Believe Me, Sweetness

Rose, Provence
Gentleness

Rose, Purple
Lust, Passion

Rose, Red
Love, Passion

Rose, Red and White
Creative force, Joy, Unity

Roses, Red with One Yellow
Excitement, Passion

Rose, Short-Stemmed
Girlhood, Sweetheart

Rose, Single
I love you, I still love you, Simplicity

Rose, Single Red
True love

Rose, Tea
I'll always remember, Remembrance

Rose, Thornless
Early attachment

Rose, White
Eternal love, False love, Heavenly, I am worthy of you,
Innocence, Purity, Secrecy, Silence

Rose, Wild
Poetry, Simplicity

Rose, Withered White
Transient Impressions

Rose, Yellow
Betrayal, Broken Heart, Decreased Love, Dying love, Forgive
and Forget, Infidelity, Intense Emotion, Jealousy

Rose, York and Lancaster
War

Rosebud
Beauty, Heart innocent of love, New love, Purity, Youth

Rosebud, Red
Pure and Lovely

Rosebud, White
Girlhood

Rosemary
Fidelity, Good luck in the New Year, Happy Marriage,
Healing, Love, Memories, Mental Powers, Protection,
Purification, Remembrance, Sleep, Success, Youth

Rosy Strife
Sports

Rowan Tree
Defense, Healing, Protection, Psychic powers, Sanctuary
Success

Rudbeckia
Impartiality, Justice

Rue
Beware of excess pleasures, Contempt, Distain, Divination,
Go, Healing, Love, Manners, Mental powers, Never return,
Emotions, Sensitivity, Self-image, Self-expression

Rushes
Calmness, Docility

Rye
Changeable disposition, Fidelity, Love

Sacred Plant
Healing

Safflower
Welcome

Saffron
Attachment, Beware of Excess, Cheerfulness, Do Not Abuse,
Foresight, Gladness, Happiness, Healing, Joviality, Love,
Lust, Mirth, Psychic Powers, Strength, Wind

Saffron, Meadow
My happiest days are past

Sage
Cherished, Comfort during mourning, Domestic Duties,
Domestic Happiness, Domestic Virtue, Esteem Immortality,

Inner Wisdom, Long Life, Longevity, New Beginnings,
Positive Perspectives, Protection, Respect, Wisdom, Wishes

Sage, Mexican
Eloquence, Spectacular

Sage, Pineapple
Esteem, Hospitality, Virtue

Sage, Purple Leaf
Gratitude

Sage Willow
Sports

Sagebrush
Absence, Encouragement, Happiness, Purification,
Tranquility

Sainfoin
Agitation, Health

Saint John's Wort
Animosity, Superstition, Divination, Happiness, Health,
Love, Power, Protection, Strength, Awareness, Reduces fears,
Superstition

Salicaire
Sports

Salvia, Blue
I think of you, Wisdom

Salvia, Red
Always yours, Forever thine, Untiring energy

Sandalwood
Healing, Protection, Spirituality

Sardony
Irony

Sarsaparilla
Love, Money

Sassafras
Health, Money

Satin Flower
Sincerity

Savory, Summer
Mental powers

Saxifrage
Balance, New ideas, Peace

Scabiosa / Pincushion Flower
Alternatives, Communication, Enthusiasm, Finding Other
Ways of Doing Something, Healing Indifference, Higher
Learning, I Have Lost All

Scorpion Grass
Forget me not

Scorpion Orchid
Elopement

Skullcap
Fidelity, Love, Peace

Sea Daffodil
Elope with me, I'm not as bad as I seem

Sea Pinks / Sea Thrift/ Sea Lavender
Sympathy

Sedum / Stonecrop
Tranquility

Seeds, Winged
Message

Sensitive Plant
Bashfulness, Sensibility, Shyness

September Flower (Aster)
Afterthought, Daintiness, Love, Variety

Sesame
Lust, Money

Shallot
Purification

Shamrock
Joy

Shasta Daisy
Patience

Shoo Fly Plant
Dignity, Pride, Success

Shooting Stars
You are my divinity

Skullcap
Calming thoughts, Letting Go

Skunk Cabbage
Legal matters

Sleeping Grass
Bashfulness, Sensibility

Slipper Orchid
Capriciousness, Catch me if you can

Slippery Elm Tree
Gossip stopper

Smilax
Loveliness

Snakeroot
Luck, Money

Snakeroot, Black
Love, Lust, Money

Snapdragon
Deception, Graciousness, No, Presumptuous, Protection, Strength, Energy, Verbal communication, You are dazzling but dangerous

Snowball
Age, Boredom, Bound, Ennui, Heaven

Snowdrop
A friend in adversity, Consolation, Hope, Spiritual confidence, Life direction, Insight, Imagination

Secret Meanings of Flowers

Snowflake
Calmness, Positive self-image

Soldier's Cap
Elegance, Fidelity, Love attraction

Solidago
Success

Solomon's Seal
Protection

Sorrel (Wood Sorrel)
Affection, Healing, Health, Joy, Not funny, Parental affection, Secret sweetness

Southernwood
Bantering

Soy Bean
Your friendship is agreeable and pleasing

Spanish Moss
Protection

Spearmint
Healing, Love, Mental Powers, Warm feelings, Warmth

Speedwell / Veronica
Facility, Fidelity, Female fidelity

Spider Flower
Elope with me, Dance with me

Spiderwort / Tradescantia
Love, Momentary happiness, Esteem but not love

Spiked Soldiers
Sports

Spiked Willow Herb
Sports

Spirea
Conceited, Victory

Spurge / Euphorbia
Welcome

Spruce Tree
Farewell, Hope in adversity, Protection

Squirrel Corn
Elegance, Fidelity, Love attraction

St. Bridgid de Caen
Delicate

Staghorn Sumac
Communication with spirit/s

Star of Bethlehem
Atonement, Hope, Idleness, Purity, Reconciliation

Starflower
Hope, Vigilance

Starwort
Afterthought, Cheerfulness in old age, Daintiness, Hospitality, Love, Variety

Statice
Dauntlessness, Gratitude, Never-ceasing, Remembrance, Success, Sympathy

Stephanotis
Good luck, Marriage, Travel, Wedding, Will you accompany me?

Stitchwort
Eases cares and worries, Relaxation, Joy

Stock
Affection, Bonds, Lasting beauty, Promptness, Vows, You will always be beautiful to me

Stonecrop/Hen and Chicks
Tranquility

Straw
Agreement, Image magic, Luck, Union

Strawflower
Agreement

Straw, Broken
Quarrel

Strawberry
Love, Luck, Perfect goodness, You are delicious, Foresight

Strawberry Tree
Faithfulness, One love

Sugar Cane
Love, Lust

Sultana
Impatience, Motherly love

Sumac
Resoluteness, Intellectual excellence

Summer Lilac
Coquetry, Evening, Virtue

Sunflower
Adoration, Devotion, Fertility, Happiness, Haughtiness, Health, Homage, Loyalty, Wisdom, Wishes

Sunflower, Dwarf
Adoration, Infatuation

Sunflower, Tall
Arrogance, Haughtiness, Pride, You are splendid

Sweet Alison/ Sweet Alyssum
Anger management, Modesty, Protection, Worth beyond beauty

Sweet Betsy
Benevolence, Generosity

Sweet Briar
Poetry

Sweet Flag
Fitness

Sweet Pea
Appointed meeting, Bliss, Blissful pleasure, Chastity, Courage, Delicate Pleasures, Departure, Friendship, Do Not Go Away, Good-bye, Let's meet, Meet me, Remember Me,

Shyness, Strength, Tenderness, Thank You for a Good Time,
Tender Memory

Sweet Rocket
Coquetry, Evening, Virtue

Sweet Shrub
Benevolence, Generosity

Sweet Sultan
Daintiness, Delicate, Felicity, Refinement

Sweet William
Artifice, Boldness, Childhood, Chivalry, Dexterity, Finesse,
Gallantry, Grant me a smile, Memories, Perfection, Scorn

Sweetbrier, Yellow
Let us forget

Sweetgrass
Spirit calling

Sweet Gum Tree
Protection

Sword Lily
Courage, Flower of the Gladiators, Generosity, Give me a
break, I'm really sincere, Love at first sight, Natural grace,
Purity, Ready-armed, Sincerity, Strength of character

Sycamore Tree
Curiosity, Genius, Reserve

Syringa, Carolina
Disappointment

Tamarind
Love

Tamarisk
Crime, Protection

Tampala
Hopelessness

Tansy
Dislike, Health, I declare war against you, I oppose you,
Longevity, Refusal, Resistance

Tea
Comfort, Courage, Gladness, Riches, Strength

Tea Rose
Always lovely

Telegraph Plant
Agitation

Texas Bluebell
Beautiful mouth, Optimistic, Outgoing, Playful, Well- spoken

Texas Mountain Laurel
Dreams, Psychic powers

Thistle
Austerity, Grief, Harshness, Healing, Independence,
Protection

Thistle, Scotch
Retaliation

Thorn Apple
Deceitful charms, Disguise, Deceit

Thrift
Sympathy

Throatwort / Trachelium
Neglected beauty

Thyme
Activity, Alluring, Courage, Energy, Healing, Health, Love, Psychic powers, Purification, Sleep

Tickseed
Cheerful, Happiness, Joy

Tiger Flower
For once may pride befriend me

Tiger Lily
Fun, I dare you to love me

Toad Flax
Deception, Presumptuous, Strength, Protection

Toadstool
Rain- making

Tobacco
Arrogance, Malevolence, Healing, Purification

Torch Lily
Dangerous, Determined

Touch Me Not
Bashfulness, Impatience, Motherly love, Sensibility

Transvaal Daisy
Beauty

Traveler's Joy
Safety

Tree of Life
Age

Trefoil
Revenge, Providence

Truffle
Surprise

Trumpet Flower
Separation

Tuberose
Pleasure, Voluptuousness

Tulip
Fame, Love, Passion, Perfect lover, Happy years, Memory

Tulip, Pink
Caring, Dreaminess

Tulip Poplar Tree
Fame

Tulip, Purple
Royalty

Tulip, Red
Believe me, Declaration of love, Love, Trust

Tulip, Variegated
Beautiful eyes

Tulip, Virgin (White)
Literary debut, Let's take a chance, Lost love

Tulip, Yellow
Hopeless love, Joy, There's sunshine in your smile

Tulip Poplar
Among the noblest, Fame, Retirement, Rural happiness

Turk's Cap
Splendor

Turmeric
Purification

Turban Buttercup
Attraction, Charm

Turnip
Charity, Ending relationships, Protection

Tussilage, Sweet-Scented
Justice shall be done

Turtlehead
Courage

Ulster Mary
Wealth

Uva Ursa
Psychic Workings

Valentine Flower
Wishes come true

Valerian
Accommodating disposition, Drunk and blousy, Facility,
Love, Protection, Purification, Purity, Sleep

Valerian, Blue
Rupture

Valerian, Red
Readiness

Vanilla
Love, Lust, Mental powers

Venus Flytrap
Artifice, Caught, Caught at last, Deceit, Love, Protection

Venus' Looking Glass
Flattery

Verbena
Enchantment, Faithfulness, Family Union, Fertility, Marriage,
Pray for Me, Tender and Quick Emotions, Will Your Wish
Be Granted?

Verbena, Lemon
Attractive to the opposite sex, Responsibility

Verbena, Purple
I will weep for you, Regret

Verbena, Scarlet
Unite against evil

Verbena, White
Honesty

Veronica
Fidelity

Vervain
Chastity, Enchantment, Healing, Love, Money, Peace,
Protection, Purification, Sleep, Youth

Vetch
Fidelity, I cling to you

Vetivert
Anti-theft, Love, Luck, Money

Tulip, Yellow
Hopeless love, Joy

Virburnum
I die if neglected, Token of affection, Thoughts of heaven

Vinca
Early friendship, Memories, Pleasures of memory, Sweet
remembrance

Vine
Drunkenness, Head over heels in love

Viola / Violet
Affection, Faith, Faithfulness, Healing, Love, Luck, Lust,
Modesty, Peace, Shyness, Watchfulness

Violet, Blue
Faithfulness, Love

Violet, Parma
Let me love you

Violet, White
Balance, Imagination, Innocence, Take a chance together

Violet, Wild
Goals, Positive outlooks, Self-understanding, Love

Violet, Yellow
Rural happiness

Virginia Creeper
I cling to you

Wake Robin
Ardor

Walking Iris
Eloquence, Faith, Friendship, Hope, Inspiration, Message,
Missive, My compliments, Passion, Promise, Valor, Wisdom,
Your friendship is valued

Wall Flower
Faithful in misfortune, Faithfulness in Adversity, Fidelity,
Friendship in Adversity

Walnut
Health, Infertility, Intellectual excellence, Intelligence, Mental powers, Strategy, Strength of mind, Wishes

Walnut Tree
Intelligence

Wandflower
Laugh at trouble

Water Lily
Eloquence, Purity, Purity of heart

Water Lily, White
Eloquence

Water Lily, Yellow
Growing indifference

Water Willow
Freedom

Watermelon
Bulk

Wax Flower
Riches

Wax Plant
Art, Protection, Sculpture, Susceptibility

Weeping Willow Tree
Disappointed in love, Divination, Emotion, Forsaken, Healing, Love, Intuition, Melancholy, Protection

Weigela
Accept a faithful heart

Wheat
Abundance, Fertility, Friendship, Friendliness, Prosperity and plenty , Riches, Worldly goods

White Hearts
Elegance, Fidelity, Love attraction

White Julienne
Despair not

White Snakeroot
Delay

Whortleberry
Treachery

Widow's Tears
Suffer from coldness

Willow Tree
Forsaken, Freedom, Friendship, Patience, Serenity

Willow Weed
Sports

Windflower / Anemone
Abandonment, Anticipation, Expectation, Love, Sincerity

Winter Gillyflower
Coquetry, Evening, Virtue

Wintergreen
Healing, Protection

Wisteria
Daughter's Sweetness, Helpless and Delicate, I Cling to Thee, Steadfast, Welcome, Welcome Fair Stranger

Witch Hazel
Chastity, Protection

Withered Flowers
Rejection

Woad
Modesty

Wolfbane
Chivalry, Invisibility, Misanthropy, Protection

Wood Sorrel
Affection, Joy, Secret Sweetness, Not funny

Woodbine
Fraternal love

Woodruff
Athletic victory, Cordiality, Money, Protection, Victory

Wormwood
Absence, Affection, Bitterness, Calling Spirits, Encouragement, Happiness, Love, Protection, Protection for Travelers, Psychic Powers, Reduces Fears, Self-determination, Tranquility

Yarrow
Courage, Cure for heartache, Healing, Heartache relief, Love War, Warning

Yew
Beginnings, Endings, Immutability, Patience, Perseverance, Renewal, Sorrow, Transitions

Yucca
Protection, Purification, Transmutation

Zephyr Flower
Expectation, Fond Caresses, Love, Sincerity

Zinnia
Absent friends, Friendship, I mourn your absence, Thoughts of absent friends

Zinnia, Magenta
Lasting affection, Affection

Zinnia, Mixed
Thinking of an absent friend, Thinking of you

Zinnia, Scarlet
Constancy, Steadfast

Zinnia, White
Goodness

Zinnia, Yellow – Daily Remembrance

Birth Month Flowers

January – Carnation or Snowdrop

February – Violet or Primrose

March – Daffodil or Jonquil

April – Daisy or Sweet Pea

May – Lily of the Valley or Hawthorn

June – Rose or Honeysuckle

July – Larkspur or Water Lily

August – Gladiolas or Poppy

September – Aster or Morning Glory

October – Calendula or Cosmos

November – Chrysanthemum

December – Narcissus or Holly

Brenda Jenkins Kleager

Anniversary Flowers

1st – Carnation
2nd – Lily of the Valley
3rd – Sunflower
4th – Hydrangea
5th – Daisy
6th – Calla Lily
7th – Freesia
8th – Lilac
9th – Bird of Paradise
10th – Daffodil
11th – Tulip
12th – Peony
13th – Chrysanthemum
14th – Orchid
15th – Rose
20th – Aster
25th – Iris
30th – Lily
40th – Gladiolus
50th – Yellow Roses and Violets

Brenda Jenkins Kleager

Plants of the Bible

Acacia
Aloe
Almond
Anise
Apple
Balm
Barley
Cattails
Cedar
Coriander
Crocus
Fig
Fir
Flax
Frankincense
Grape
Grass
Hazel
Hyssop
Lilies
Lintels
Millet
Mustard Seed
Myrtle
Narcissus
Olive
Palm
Pine
Pomegranate

Poppy
Rue
Spelt
Sycamore
Tulip
Vines
Wheat

COLOR THEORY

Colors can affect emotions and mood. When in doubt about what flowers you would like to select for specific purposes, a quick and rather dependable strategy is to use color theory.

Some colors have the same associations due to cultural differences and sources consulted.

The following list is a guide and may not be complete. Use it as a starting point for your explorations of flower colors.

Black: Protection, wisdom, infinity, death, rebirth
Blue-Black: Wounded pride
Blue: Truth, wisdom, peace, poetry
Brown- Calmness, earth, security, support
Gray- Sorrow, friendship, maturity, responsibility
Green – Healing, forest, youth, hope, new beginnings, abundance, money
Gold- Wealth, optimism, good health
Indigo- Wisdom, spirituality
Lavender- Peace, charity, dreams, serenity
Orange- Creativity, happiness, opportunities, power
Pink- Friendship, remembrance, beauty, harmony
Red – Passion, courage, strength, life, faith, action
Silver – Freedom, reality, restoration, endurance
Violet- Truth, justice, intelligence, humility, religion, forgiveness
White – Purity, kindness
Yellow- Intelligence, healing, intuition, light, life, creativity

Brenda Jenkins Kleager

FLOWERS AND PLANTS
FOR
SPECIAL OCCASIONS

Use these suggestions as starting points for selecting flowers and plants for specific occasions. Find additional florals that would be just as appropriate within the section of meanings.

Select just one flower for a single effect, or mix the flowers for aesthetics or to convey deeper emotions. You will want to consider the colors and aspects of each flower if you are mixing the flowers for a bouquet or tussie-mussie.

You may consider including a copy of this book with the flowers you give so that the recipient will know your intent.

Anniversary Celebration (any) – Impatiens, Iris, Arum, Red Carnations

Ancestor Honoring – White Dahlia, Clematis, Evergreen Sprigs, Crown Imperial, Vinca

Belated Birthday – White Daisies, Purple Hyacinth

Birth of a Girl – Oregano, Lotus, Pink Carnations, English Daisies

Birth of a Boy – Oregano, Lotus, Nasturtiums, English Daisies, Lily of the Valley

Birthday to a Friend – Coreopsis, Jasmine, Peppermint, Abor Vitae, Oak-leaf Geranium, Roses, Crocus, Chrysanthemums, Sage, Lavender, Peach, Figs, Maple Tree (See **Friendship**)

Birthday to a Lover – Mums, Sage, Fern, Daffodils, Red Roses, Asters, Lilacs, Rose of Sharon, Violets

Bon Voyage – Zinnias, Cyclamen, Sweet Pea, Persian Violet, Mint, Lucky Hand

Breaking Up – Pinks, Lilies, Turnips, Anemone, Rue, Ice Plant, Sweet Pea, Skullcap, Yellow Carnations

Bridal Shower – Oranges, Holly

Consolation for any Loss – Snowdrop, Red Poppy

Creative Endeavors - Clematis, Basil

Engagements – Basil, Red Carnation, Grape Hyacinth, White Tulips, Honeysuckle, Holly, Ambrosia, Dogwood, Mums, Yellow Tulips, Almonds, Iris, Phlox, Arbutus, Bellflower

Father's Day – Bougainvillea, Lilac, Honeysuckle

First Car or New Car – Azalea, Oleander, Caladium, Sunflower, Coreopsis, Eryngo

Funeral Flowers – Helenium, Purple Hyacinths, Cyclamen, White Roses, Heliotrope, Orange Blossom, Evergreen Sprigs, Bluebell, Yellow Iris, Purple Hyacinth

Get Well - Pears, Scarlet Geranium, Feverfew, Cotton, Columbine, Rosemary (See **Healing and Health**)

Good-bye – Sweet Pea, Morning Glory, Forget-Me-Not, Cyclamen, Spruce Tree, Datura, Carolina Jasmine, Striped Carnation

Good Luck in School – Hollyhock, Ivy, Cherry Blossom, Clover, Scabiosa

Graduation Congratulations – African Violet, Yellow Carnations

Heartache Relief – Red Camellias, Red Carnations, Yellow Roses, Yarrow, Cranberry, Marigold, Aloe, Morning Glory, Achillea, Butterfly Weed, Yarrow, Lavender

Honoring Ancestors – Guelander Rose, Bougainvillea

Hostess Gift – Fuchsia, Jasmine

I Love You – Red Tulips, Althea, Peaches, Single Red Rose, Red Chrysanthemum, Almonds, Cosmos, Mandevilla (See **Love**)

I'm Sorry – Purple Hyacinths, Red Poppies

Infatuation or Beginning a New Relationship – Fern, Periwinkles, Purple Lilies, Lavender Roses, Coreopsis, Bleeding Heart, Ox-eye Daisy, Rosebud, Apple-scented Geranium

Lovers' Tryst/Secret Love – Almonds, Maidenhair Fern, Gardenia, Beech Tree, Pimpernel, Yellow Chrysanthemum, Mimosa Tree

Mother's Day – Pussy Willow, Lilies, Amaryllis

New Business Wishes – Azalea, Mums, Bellflowers, Hollyhocks, Buttercups, Clover

New Home Joy - Juniper

New Job Luck – Parsley, Rue, Pimpernel, Clover, Dusty Miller, Apple Blossom, Camellia, Moss, Poppies, Sage

Passionate Love – Delphinium, Bearded Iris, Prickly Pear, Red Camellia, Red Poppy, Purple Roses, Orange Roses, Tulips, Camellias, Althea (Rose of Sharon)

Prom – White Carnation (male), Chrysanthemum, Daisy, Lily, Fressia

Promotion in Rank or Business – Lobelia, Gueleder Rose

Recovery After Serious Illness or Surgery – Holly, primroses, Cypress Tree, Pine Tree, Violets (See **Healing** and **Health**)

Retirement – Gueleder Rose, Snowball, Fern

School Luck – Walnut Tree or Walnuts, Daisies, Sage, Yew, Magnolia, Coral Bells, Cymbidium Orchid, Hollyhock (See **Wisdom**)

Soldiers' Service Recognition – Cardinal Flower, laurel, Tulip Poplar Tree, Peony, Cactus, Oak Leaves, Pine Tree, Holly, Lobelia, Lantana, Columbine

Sporting Events Success – Tansy, Laurel, Thyme, Basil, Woodruff, Hollyhock, Day Lily, Carnations, Coral Bells, Fern, Columbine, Willow Weed, Foxtail, Hyacinth, Cedar, Snapdragon, Spirea

Sweet Sixteen Celebration – Wisteria, Mayflower, Crocus, White Lilac

Sympathy – Yarrow, Lilac, Moon Vine, Lisianthus, Bee Balm, Red Poppy, Aloe, Marigold, Yarrow, Cypress Tree, Dark Crimson Rose, Yew

Thank You – Parsley, Sage, Statice, Camellia, Deep Pink Rose, Fleabane, Deep Pink Roses, Sweet Peas

Young Love / Affection – Ivy, Jonquil, Violets, Celosia, Zinnias, Anemone, Damask Rose, Purple Lilacs

Wedding / Marriage – Sage, Coxcomb, Bridal Wreath, Pea, Magenta Zinnias, Phlox, Morning Glory, Stock, Carnation, Daisies, Mums, Mimosa Tree, Periwinkle, Straw, Ivy, Stephanotis

Welcome to my Home / Hospitality – Peppermint, Woodruff, Oak, Pineapple, Euphorbia, Safflower

Brenda Jenkins Kleager

BIBLIOGRAPHY

Print Resources:

Cunningham, Scott. *Magical Herbalism*. St. Paul, MN: Llewellyn Publications. 2001.

Cunningham, Scott. *The Magic In Food: Legends, Lore & Spellwork*. St. Paul, MN: Llewellyn Publications. 1990.

Dover Publications. *Flower Designs and Motifs*. Mineola, NY: Dover Publications. 2005.

Eerman, Matthias (translated by Grace Jackman). *Wild Flowers*. New York: Galahad Books. 1993.

Holland, Eileen. *Holland's Grimoire of Magickal Correspondences: A Ritual Handbook*. Franklin Lakes, NJ: The Career Press. 2006.

Hopman, Ellen Everet. *A Druid's Herbal for the Sacred Earth Year*. Rochester, VT: Destiny Books. 1995.

Kynes, Sandra. *Whispers from the Woods*. Woodbury, MN: Llewellyn Publications. 2006.

Laufer, Geraldine Adamich. *Tussie-Mussies: The Victorian Art of Expressing Yourself in the Language of Flowers*. New York: Workman Publishing. 1993.

Lust, John. *The Herb Book*. New York: Bantam Books. 1983.

Meyer, Joseph E. *The Herbalist and Herb Doctor*. Hammond, IN: Indiana Botanic Gardens. 1934.

Pickles, Shelia. *The Language of Flowers: Penhaligon's Scented Treasury of Verse and Prose*. New York: Harmony Books. 1990.

Seaton, Beverly. *The Language of Flowers*. Virginia: The University Press of Virginia. 1995.

Vitale, Alice Thomas. *Leaves in Myth, Magic and Medicine*. New York: Barnes and Noble. 1997.

Internet Resources:

http://www.iflorist.com/en/gifts/meaning/

http://www.aboutflowers.com/floral_b5.html

http://www.teleflora.com/flowercolors.asp

http://www.links2love.com/flowers_meanings_pictures.htm

http://www.vietfun.com/flowers

http://www.languageofflowers.com/flowermeaning.htm#anchora

http://home.comcast.net/`bryant.katherine/flwrmeanings.html

http://www.complete-herbal.com/culpepper.html

http://www.photovault.com/Link/Food/PlantsHerbsSymbolism.html

http://www.greenmantrees.demon.co.uk/flower.html#

http://www.literarycalligraphy.com/books/history.html

http://www.victorianbazaar.com/meanings.html

http://www.whats-your-sign.com/flowers-and-meanings.html

http://www.online-literature.com/shakespeare/hamlet/17/

http://www.ehow.com/list_7600324_flowers-used-heraldry.html. "Flowers Used in Heraldry" by Jacquelyn Jeanty.

http://cultureandcommunication.org/deadmedia/index.php/Language_of_Flowers

http://garden.lovetoknow.com/wiki/Roses_and_Their_Meaning

http: victorianbazar.com/meanings.html

http://www.quotegarden.com/flowers.html

http://www.nurserymanagementonline.com/Article.aspx?article_id=128745

http://www.marshallparthenon.com/americans-spend-too-much-money-on-valentine-s-day-1.2700388#.URlLPsWQnKQ

http://www.crystal-cure.com/orange.html

http://www.ehow.com/info_8071924_flowers-plants-bible.html

http://search.yahoo.com/search?fr=mcafee&p=flowers+of+the+Bible

http://books.google.com/books/about/Flowers_of_the_Bible.html?id=PVS4ZCp3AkoC

ABOUT THE AUTHOR

Brenda's father taught high school Biology, Chemistry and Physics. Spending a few hours with him in the backyard was an incredible science lesson, imbued with the awe of nature itself and its mysticism. It is through him that she gained her lifelong interest in our natural world.

In addition to writing and nature, Brenda's interests include genealogy, quilting, photography and scrapbooking.

Brenda grew up in Madison (Nashville), Tennessee and currently lives in northern Alabama with her husband, two cats and a dog. She enjoys long weekends and family vacations at their lake house in Kentucky.

Contact her at brendakleager@yahoo.com

Visit her website at treasuredsecretspublishing.com for news about this book as well as her next book, *Secret Meanings of Gemstones*.

Join her for more fun facts, questions and answers, in addition to discussions about plants and their meanings at the Yahoo group, flower-meanings.

Brenda Jenkins Kleager

Made in the USA
Middletown, DE
13 January 2017